EMPOWERMENT OF WOMEN THROUGH POLITICAL PARTICIPATION

EMPOWERMENT OF WOMEN THROUGH POLITICAL PARTICIPATION

By

Dr. (Mrs.) Niroj Sinha

KALPAZ

Published by

Kalpaz Publications
C-30, Satyawati Nagar,
Delhi – 110052
Ph.: 011-47034999, 9811692060
www.kalpazpublications.com
E-mail: kalpaz@hotmail.com

Distribution Network
gyanbooks.com
India, USA, Canada, UK, Australia, France

ISBN: 978-81-7835-345-6 (HB)

Reprint in India, 2024
First Published, 2013

Printed at: Gyan Press, Delhi.

Empowerment of Women Through Political Participation
Author: Dr. (Mrs.) Niroj Sinha

Contents

Preface

The importance of women's political participation for a viable Democratic Polity is being increasingly realized in all corners of the world. Women constitute nearly 50 percent of the total population in any Country and if it has adopted a democratic system it cannot run successfully with just half of the population. It will be a crippled Democracy. Moreover, women as a group have problems, demands and aspirations which cannot be aptly expressed by men. The problem issues of the people in any country such as, education, employment, health and nutrition besides the country's foreign policy, relationships with other countries, issues of war and peace, science and technology, protection of the environment do need a women's angle because they will affect women too, in a particular manner. But a glimpse at the world scenario gives us the grim picture that barring a couple of exceptions, most of the Parliaments have 93 per cent male representatives and just 7 per cent are women, give or take one or two per cent. The World Congress of women at Beijing in 1995 reiterated the importance of increasing women's participation in Politics and in its "Platform of Action" recommended ways and means to the participating countries to increase "space for and visibility" of women in political institutions and processes. This is the important first step towards women's empowerment.

The degree and level of women's participation in politics however, differs from country to country and even in the different regions of the same country, especially in a country like India where regional variations regarding levels of development, urbanization education are massive. Therefore, studied of women's political participation need to be related to their particular regional environment—the socio-cultural and economic environment.

The present study has been conducted in the regional context of composite Bihar. Composite Bihar has been the second most populous state in India, and has also influenced national politics to a great extent. However, this state records a very low status of women in terms of education, employment and health. The urbanisation ratio of the state is very low and feudal values are persisting with a vengeance directing its social, economic and political structures. The feudal values tend to throttle the development of women specifically, and with lowest female literacy, poverty and poor health, how can women of Bihar play a vital and dynamic role in State and national politics ? Hence, this Research Project.

I am thankful to the University Grants Commission, New Delhi, for generously providing funds for this project. Without their grant, this study would never have been possible, and a much needed area of social research as regards Bihar would have been neglected.

My thanks are due to my field investigators Sri Ghanshyam Roy and Ms Chanchala Kumari for their diligent and hard work in collecting relevant data and also for providing me with secondary data from the various Libraries. I also thank Ms Sushila Sinha for tabulation and coding of the relevant data.

My thanks are due to the Library, center for Women's Development Studies, New Delhi, Library of the National Commission on Women, New Delhi, Library of Election Commission, New Delhi, A.N. Sinha Institute Library, Patna, Sinha Library and Bihar Vidhan Sabha Library, Patna. I am especially obliged to Dr. Prabhash Prasad Singh, Assistant Librarian, A.N. Sinha Institute Library, for his Cooperation in providing me with relevant reports and reading materials, and also for his valuable suggestions in analysis of data and writing of the Report.

Niroj Sinha

1

Introduction

It is a global experience that women play a marginal role in politics. Their presence in political structures is almost invisible barring a few countries such as the Nordic Countries where it is above 40 per cent in the State Legislatures. Even though Democracy has made great gains in the 1990's women average only 11.6 per cent of the World Legislatures (Report of the Inter-Parliamentary Union 1997) Women essentially are appointed by men in at least 37 undemocratic countries or are entirely missing from the National Legislatures. In an additional 49 nations—the new democracies or the partially developed ones—men parliamentarians dominate the legislature with 93 per cent membership. Only in the 27 long-standing democracies do women have the greatest opportunity for equality in representation yet women members of even these parliaments average only 15 per cent.[1] Government of the people, by the people and for the people—Abraham Lincoln's concept of Democracy—is an ideal which remains unachieved in the World especially in the context of half the population of the World—the women.

Indian Democracy is more than fifty years old now yet the ideals of Democracy are far from destination as ever—especially for women in India. Indian population is made up of various groups organized around different issues such as religion, race, caste ethnicity, language, region put the largest formation cutting across all these issues is gender based—it is of women who form almost 50 per cent of the total population.

It is imperative to asks what these 50 odd years have given to women. Despite their number they are marginal in all spheres of life. The marginalisation of groups around caste and to some extent class has been recognized from the initial stages of Independence, and special efforts have been made to redress these imbalances, but nothing much has been done for women, especially in the context of their marginalisation in politics. The Statute Books are well replete with provisions regarding political rights (perhaps gained with less effort than her counterparts in other countries), yet the reality presents a grim picture. Women have been unable to create "political space", for themselves.[2] They have not been able even to project themselves as an important and viable "Vote Bank".

In the last few years, there has been considerable emphasis on Political Participation as the most important vehicle for the empowerment of women in public-private meetings, seminars, discussions, debates among the academics on the one hand and the activists on the other. The Beijing Conference in 1995 reiterated this issue in its "Platform for Action" and urged the members from participating states to take up the issue of marginalisation of women in political structures and processes in their own countries very seriously and devise ways and means to increase the "Visibility and Space" for women in the democratic processes of their respective countries. An agenda was drawn up especially for Political Parties to create 'space' for women in their party structures because in a democratic government parties are the main instrument for ensuring the entry of individuals in the Governmental bodies. While things did improve in some countries, but in India, the percentage of women who won the Lok Sabha Elections in 1996, did not go beyond 8 per cent. It has not improved even in the later Lok Sabha elections of 1998 and 1999 (Table 1).

TABLE 1

Women in Lok Sabha (1952-1999)

Lok Sabha		*Seats*	*Women Candidates*	*Elected*
1952	I	499	51 (2.7%)	22 (4.9%)
1957	II	500	70 (5.5%)	27 (5.4%)
1962	III	503	68 (3.4%)	34 (6.7%)
1967	IV	523	66 (2.8%)	31 (5.9%)

(Contd.)

(Contd. Table 1)

1971	V	544	86(3.1%)	22 (4.2%)
1977	VI	521	70 (2.9%)	19(3.4%)
1980	VII	544	142(3.1%)	28 (5.0%)
1984	VIII	544	159(2.9%)	44 (7.7%)
1989	IX	517	189(3.1%)	27 (5.3%)
1991	X	544	195(3.7%)	39 (6.7%)
1996	XI	543	191 (3.4%)	39(7.1%)
1998	XII	543	167(3.0%)	43 (7.9%)
1999	XIII	513	284(6.1%)	49 (9.7%)

Source: General Elections to Lok Sabha—Statistical Reports Election Commission, New Delhi.

The traditional norms regarding women's activities have been carried generation to generation unquestioningly. The thinking that political activities belong to the "Public Sphere" and women by nature and inclination belong to the "Private Sphere" has been harped on continuously and has socialized women to perceive "Politics" as something 'alien' to their nature. The debate on the 'Capabilities' issues are linked with women and not with other marginalized groups such as especially "Caste groups" in Indian society. When particular castes are mobilized, given reservation, and made visible in the political arena, issues of their capability, awareness, education are set aside, but when a marginalized group based on gender demands space, a myriad of questions are put up. We have experienced several instances of turmoil, even violent outbursts against the passage of 33 per cent Reservation Bill for women in Lok Sabha and State Assemblies. In the case of other groups it is directly related to values of Democracy, but not in the case of women.[3]

However, if we believe at all in Democracy, we have to accept that it can be viable only if the whole population is ensured access to its processes and structures. A Democracy working with just 50 per cent of the population can never be accepted as a strong and viable system of governance. Women have to be given access and space in the political arena and the issue of their training, awareness, has to be taken up and tackled with great effort, gender sensitivity and sincerity.

While looking at issues related to women, one has to keep caution in mind—it is necessary to understand that women do not form a homogeneous groups. There are various sub-groups among the women based on different issues of caste, class, religion, ethnicity, levels of development etc., which affect the behaviour pattern of members of the group. Second, the regional setting also plays an important role. As situations differ from country to country, so do they differ from region to region within a country. A country like India has various regional variations State to State, and even within one state. The historical, social, economic, cultural and geographical factors play very decisive roles in shaping the behaviour of individuals. Similarly, women are affected by their environmental set up while playing their political roles. In India we have States like Kerala and Maharashtra showing indexes of higher level of women's status, whereas we have States like Bihar, Madhya Pradesh, Orissa, Uttar Pradesh which record a very low status of women. While examining the level and viability of the political activities of women, these factors have to be taken into account. Even for preparing an agenda for improvement in the state of affairs and devising infrastructures for implementing action plans into reality, we have to take into consideration these factors.

Women and Political Participation in Bihar

Bihar is one of the most backward regions (State) of India in general and in the context of women's status in particular. The socio-economic and educational status of women in this state is very low, much below the national average. Women in Bihar are by and large poor and illiterate, bound by age-old customs and traditions. Further they are surrounded by an environment of violence and crime. How does she fare in politics in this hostile environment of feudal backwardness, domination and crime and violence? Not much has been written and documented about women's political activities in Bihar. It is a much needed area of study and research. It is important also because Bihar has been the second most populous state in India till very recent past (15.11.2000). Democracy as a form of government requires the participation of more and more citizens, to whatever groups they may belong to become strong and viable. The quality of political participation of women of Bihar is not only important for this State only, but also for the whole nation. Therefore, this research project "Empowerment of women through political participation: Study of Women's political participation in Bihar" is being undertaken to make a detailed enquiry into the political role and activities of women in Bihar, to identify the socio-economic educational factors which present hurdles in the way of women's meaningful and quality political participation, to plan strategies for the betterment of women's political status.

While discussing women's political participation in Bihar, it should be taken into account from the very outset that Bihari women have played a very important role in various political movements, although their presence in political structures is not very visible.

It would be appropriate here to analyze the current meaning of politics and political participation. Traditionally, political participation is limited to participation in formal political structures the Legislatures, Executive in a democratic set up. It has now been widened by political theorists to include movements, protests and struggles as legitimate expressions of political behaviour.

Feminist scholar have challenged the dominant hypothesis that 'politics' is confined to public sphere. They maintain that traditional politics legitimizes women's exclusion or absence from power spheres and also devalues women's concerns.[4]

Women's participation in formal political structures will be analyzed with the help of empirical data in later chapters, women's participation in political movements is not included in this particular study. A short review of women's activities as voters, contestants, members of Legislature, Parliament, Council of Ministers is being made from 1952 to the present. Since political activities happen within the socio-economic and cultural environment of the individuals, the chapter on Bihar later, will give a synoptic view of the situational context of political participation of women of Bihar. Suffice it to mention here that the economic, educational and social status of women in Bihar is very low nearly 25 million women are illiterate. According to NSS organization survey of July '93 there are just 155 women engaged in some sort of work as in every 1000. Added to all this is the low pace of urbanization which aids feudal values to persists and the culture of relentless violence.[5]

Mobilisation of Women as Voters—Lok Sabha

The voting percentage of women on an all India basis reflects the sad fact that Bihar has been one among the five states which have had lowest mobilization of women voters for a long period. While the percentage of voter turn out for the first two General Election is not available, the record of 1962 Elections shows that the ratio of women voters in Bihar was just 32.96 per cent as compared to Kerala's 67.70 per cent. The table will amplify that women in Bihar have not been properly mobilized even as voters to date although Bihar does not feature amongst the five lowest mobiliser States of women voters after 1984.

In 1967, Bihar's percentage was 40.70 as against Kerala's 74.20. The ratio declined again in 1971 with 37.74 as against Tamil Nadu's 69.17. The number of female voters had exceeded from 6633754 in 1952 to 20526493 in 1984. In two parliamentary constituencies of Ranchi and Khunti, women voters outnumbered the males respectively by 27141 and 2218. The percentage dropped to 38.17 in '91 as against Lakshdweep's 85.48 per cent. The percentage has improved to 50.40 in '96, 55.83 in '98 and in '99 (Table 2).

TABLE 2

Bihari Women's Participation in Lok Sabha Polls 1962-1999

Year	*Bihar*	*%*	*Highest in India*	*%*
1962	Bihar	32.96	Kerala	67.08
1967	"	40.74	Kerala	74.20
1971	"	37.01	Tamil Nadu	69.17
1977	"		Kerala	79.61
1980	"	43.91	West Bengal	68.18
1984	"	49.18	Manipur	90.00
1989	"	50.25	Lakshdweep	89.30
1991	"	38.17	Lakshdweep	85.38
1996	"	50.40	Lakshdweep	11.35
1998	"	55.83	Lakshdweep	87.70
1999	"	53.33	Lakshdweep	83.41

Sources: Culled from Reports of General Elections to Lok Sabha, Election Commission of India, New Delhi.

The sad fact is that Bihar presents a picture of persistently low mobilization in absolute terms and also in relation to men. In the case of Bihar, it is very easy to correlate it with the socio-economic indicators of development. Women are illiterate (every 8th illiterate women in India is from Bihar), poor, the culture is basically rural ensuring the severe restrictive hold of feudal values on society — a society which has always seen women as secondary. So, low literacy, health and nutrition, poverty, predominantly rural culture with the absence of Industrial Development and Urban Growth combine together to strengthen feudal traditions which relegate women to a secondary position and confine her to the world of private sphere/family.

Mobilisation of Women Voters—Vidhan Sabha

Sexwise ratio of voters in Bihar Vidhan Sabha elections was not available till recently. In 1980 General Elections the percentage of women voters was 38.50 as against the male's 61.42. The difference in percentage between the males and females was 22.84. In the 1985 elections, the percentage of women voters was 38.41 as against the males 61.59, the difference being 23.18 per cent. In 1995, the percentage of women voters was 42.58 as against the male's 57.41 per cent. The gap had narrowed a little—to 14.83 per cent. In year 2000, the percentage of women voters was 39.78 as against the male's 60.21 and the percentage difference again increased to 20.43 (Table 3).

TABLE 3

Mobilisation of Women and Men Voters for Bihar Vidhan Sabha Election 1980-2000

Year	*Male*	*Female*	*Diff. %*
1980	61.42	38.50	22.84
1985	61.59	38.41	23.18
1990	NB	NB	NB
1995	57.41	42.58	14.83
2000	60.21	3978	2043

Soutce: Reports of General Elections to Bihar Vidhan Sabha: Statistical Analysis.

Membership in Lok Sabha

Bihar till recently (before the creation of Jharkhand State on 15.11.2000) was the second most populous state of the Indian Union and had 54 seats in the 543 membered Lok Sabha. Presently Bihar has just 36 seats while Jharkhand has 18 seats in Lok Sabha. History shows that the number of women from Bihar in Lok Sabha registered a steady increase between 1952 and 1984. From two in '52 it rose to 9 in '84. In the second Lok Sabha there were five members from Bihar. Tarkeshwari Sinha, Shakuntala Devi and Satyabhama Devi won on Congress ticket while Lalita Rajyalakshmi and Vijaya Raje were nominees of the Janata Party of Ramgarh house. Both of them along with a third member of the family, Ms Shashank Manjari got re-elected to the third Lok Sabha (1962) on the then Swatantra Party ticket, to raise the total number of Bihari MP's to seven. The MP's from Congress Party were Tarkeshwari Sinha, Shakuntala Devi, Satyabhama Devi and Ramdulari Sinha. The 4th Lok Sabha (1967) witnessed a decline in the numbers. The total was 4,—two from Congress were Tarkeshwari Sinha and Kamala Kumari where as Lalita Rajyalakshmi and Vijay Raje won as Independents. The Vth Lok Sabha (1971) had just one Bihari MP—Kamala Kumari. Six women fought elections for 6th Lok Sabha (1977) and all of them lost. The Seventh Lok Sabha (1980) saw six women from Bihar. Nine known women fought election, out of which four won. They were Ramdulari Sinha, Kamala Kumari, Krishna Shahi and Madhuri Singh. The other two were new faces in Lok Sabha—Kishori Sinha won on the Janata ticket while Sumati Oraon came to Lok Sabha after the death of her husband, Kartik Oraon. The 8th Lok Sabha (1984) saw the largest contingent of women MPs from Bihar—a total of nine. All the sitting six MPs were returned to the Lok Sabha with one slight change—Kishori Sinha won on Congress ticket this time. The three new faces were Prabhawati Gupta, (then a minister in Bihar) Chandrabhanu Devi and Manorama Singh from Congress I. In the 9th Lok Sabha the number decreased to just 2.

In 1991 three women went to the 10th Lok Sabha—Rita Verma from BJP, Dr. Girija Pandey on Janata Dal ticket and Krishna Shahi on Congress I ticket. In 1996 the number remained constant at three with Rita Verma getting re-elected. Kanti Singh and

Bhagwati Devi won on Janata Dal ticket. In 1998 once against Rita Verma won for the third time. Another BJP nominee was Abha Mahto, Kanti Singh and Malti Devi won on RJD ticket.

In 1999 (13th Lok Sabha) Rita Verma and Abha Mahto repeated their success once again on BJP ticket. Others who won were Renu Kumari (JDU), Shyama Singh (Inc) and Kanti Singh (RJD) (Table 4).

TABLE 4

Gender Composition of Lok Sabha 1952-99 (Special Reference to Bihar)

Year	*Total no. of seats*	*Total no. % of women*	*Total No. women from Bihar*
1952	499	22 (4.4)	2
1957	500	27 (5.4)	5
1962	503	34 (6.8)	7
1967	523	31 (5.9)	4
1971	544	19 (3.4)	1
1977	521	22 (4.2)	Nil
1980	544	28 (7.8)	6
1984	544	44 (8.1)	9
1989	517	27 (5.3)	2
1991	544	36 (7.2)	3
1996	543	39 (7.2)	3
1998	543	43 (7.91)	4
1999	*513*	*49 (9.7)*	5

Source: Cullen from various Statistical Reports of General Elections to Lok Sabha—Election Commission—New Delhi.

In all 50 women have gone to Lok Sabha from Bihar from 1952 to 1991 (List in Appendix-1). Party-wise the women of Congress Party have fared better in the earlier elections till 1984, excepting 1971 and 1977. In the recent four elections of the present decade, BJP and Janata Dal and after the split RJD have been able to send women to Lok Sabha. The '99 Lok Sabha saw just one women win on Congress ticket, the daughter-in-law of Satyendra Narain Sinha, Shyama Singh. In the Janata "wave" leaders like Krishna Shahi from Congress Party had to loose election.

One feature that stands out is that many women MPs from Bihar have repeated their success both in the past and also at present. Names like Tarkeshwari Sinha, Satyabhama Devi, Kamla Kumari, Ramdulari Sinha, Krishna Shahi stands out in the first three decades after the 1st Lok Sabha started working. In the '90s we have the example of Rita Verma successfully entering the Lok Sabha for the 4th time in '99. Close on heels is Abha Mahto, Rita Verma is now a Cabinet Minister in the Union Government. Kanti Singh also has her own success story to recall. She also was Union Cabinet Minister for Coal. Earlier, Krishna Shahi, Ramdulari Sinha had successful tenures as Ministers. Nonetheless, the name of Tarkeshwari Sinha has always to be remembered as the 'fireband' from Bihar for her exemplary oration as a parliamentarian in three Lok Sabha tenure. She has been the only women Deputy Finance Minister to date.

Despite the backwardness of the State, women from Bihar have performed satisfactorily in Lok Sabha. Majority of the women MPs from Bihar have had a very sound education, exposure to public life, grasp of issues of public interest.

Membership in Vidhan Sabha

While the number of women from Bihar to Lok Sabha did register a rise at times, it has been declining sharply in the Vidhan Sabha after 1967 General Elections.[6] From fourteen in 1952 it rose upto 34 in 1957 only to come down to 25 in 1962.[7] Since 1967 the number has never exceeded 13 in a house of 324 members. The Fourth Vidhan Sabha (1967) had eleven women which went down to 4 in 1969. In 1972, the total again rose to eleven with a slight increase of one in 1977, '80[8] and three in '85.[9] In the '85 elections, 13 out of a hundred women contestants in run were successful. Eleven has won on Congress I ticket which had set up 32 candidates, one each have come from CPI and Dalit Majdoor Kisan Party (DMKP). The Janata Party had put up five women candidates but drew a blank.[10] It again decreased to 13 in 1990 and 11 in 1995. The present Vidhan Sabha has nineteen women members, out of which two have gone to Jharkhand after the creation of the new State of Jharkhand (Table 5) here.

TABLE 5

Gender Composition of Women in Bihar Vidhan Sabha and Vidhan Parishad 1952-2000

	Vidhan Parishad				*Vidhan Sabha*	
Year	*Total no. of seats 324*	*Total no. of female contestants*	*Total no. and % women*	*Total seats 96*	*Year*	*Total No.*
1952			13 (4.01)		1952	4(4.16)
1957			34 (10.49)		1957	3(3.12)
1962			25 (7.71)		1962	7 (7.29)
1967			12 (3.70)		1967	8(8.3)
1969			4 (1.23)		1972	5 (5.20)
1972			11(3.39)		1977	8 (8.3)
1977		89	12 (3.70)		1980	5 (5.20)
1980		76	11 (3.39)		1985	6 (6.25)
1985		100	14 (4.32)		1990	5 (5.20)
1990		—	13 (4.01)		1996	—
1995		264	11 (3.39)		1998	4(4.16)
2000		188	19(5.86)			

Source: I *Origin and Development of Bihar Legislature* (ed.) Radha Nandan Jha, Speaker Bihar Vidhan Sabha, Printed at Text Book Press Patna 1—For 1952-1977.

II For 1980, 85, 95-2000—Reports of Bihar Legislative Assembly Elections—Statistical Analysis. Election Commission—Bihar.

III *Hindustan* (daily newspaper), Patna dated 12.12.1998. For Vidhan Sabha.

The percentage of women MLA's in Bihar stands at the State average of 4.3 as against the highest 6.2 in the State of Haryana. The State-wise average of women contestants in State Assembly elections from 1952-97 shows that for Bihar the average of contestants per seat is 0.20 and the success ratio in '95 was 16.7 per cent (Table 6 & 7).

TABLE 6

Women's Representation in State Legislature 1952-1997 (Percentage of Women MLAs)

States	*1952***	*1957*	*1960-65*	*1967-69*	*1970-75*	*1977-78*	*1979-83*	*1984-88*	*1989-92*	*1993 97*	*State Avg.*
Andhra Pradesh	2.9	3.7	3.3	3.8	9.1	3.4	4.1	3.4	3.7	2.7	4.0
Arunachal Pradesh	—	—	—	—	—	0.0	3.3	6.7	33	3.3	3.3
Assam	0.5	4.6	3.8	4.0	7.0	0.8	0.8	4.0	4.0	4.8	3.2
Bihar	3.6	9.4	7.9	2.2*	3.8	4.0	3.7	4.6	2.8	3.4	4.3
Goa	—	—	—	6.7	3.3	3.3	0.0	0.0	5.0	10.0	4.3
Gujarat	—	—	8.4	4.8	3.2	NE	2.7	8.8	2.2	1.1	4.2
Haryana	—	—	—	7.4*	6.2	4.4	7.8	5.6	6.7	4.4	6.2
Himachal Pradesh	0.0	—	—	0.0	5.9	1.5	4.4	4.4	5.9	4.4	3.6
Jammu & Kashmir	—	NE	0.0	0.0	5.3	1.3	0.0	1.3	NE	2.3	1.5
Karnataka	2.0	8.7	8.7	3.2	5.1	4.0	0.9	3.6	4.5	3.1	4.5
Kerala	0.0	4.8	3.9*	0.8	1.5	0.7	3.2	5.7	5.7	9.3	3.6
Madhya Pradesh	2.1	10.8	4.9	3.4	5.4	3.1	5.6	9.7	3.4	3.8	5.1
Maharashtra	1.9	6.3	4.9	3.3	9.3	2.8	6.6	5.6	2.1	3.8	4.7
Manipur	—	NE	NE	0.0	0.0*	NE	0.0	0.0	1.7	0.0	0.3
Meghalaya	—	—	—	—	1.7	1.7	0.0	3.3	NE	1.7	1.7
Mizoram	—	—	—	—	0.0	3.3	3.3	2.5	0.0	0.0	1.4
Nagaland	—	—	0.0	0.0	NE	0.0	0.0	1.7	0.0	0.0	0.5
Orissa	9.6	3.6	1.4	3.6	1.4*	4.8	3.4	6.1	4.8	5.4	4.0
Punjab	2.2	5.8	5.2	1.0*	5.8	2.6	5.1	3.4	5.1	6.0	4.0
Rajasthan	0.0	5.1	4.5	3.3	7.1	4.0	5.0	8.0	5.5	4.5	4.8
Sikkim	—	—	—	—	—	—	0.0	0.0	6.3	3.1	2.3
Tamil Nadu	0.3	5.9	3.9	1.7	2.1	0.9	2.1	3.4	9.0	3.8	3.6
Tripura	—	NE	NE	0.0	3.3	1.7	6.7	3.3	NE	1.7	3.0
Uttar Pradesh	1.2	5.8	4.4	2.8*	5.9	2.6	5.6	7.3	3.3*	4.0*	4.1
West Bengal	0.8	3.6	4.8	2.9	1.6*	1.4	2.4	4.4	7.1	6.8	3.4
Delhi	4.2	—	NE	NE	7.1	7.1	7.1	NE	NE	4.3	5.9
Pondicherry	—	—	6.7	3.3	0.0	0.0	3.3	3.3	1.7	3.3	2.6
Period Average	1.8	6.3	4.9	2.9	4.4	2.8	3.8	5.3	4.5	4.0	4.0

TABLE 7

Women Contestants in State Assembly Elections: State-wise Averages 1952-1996

States	*Contestants Per seat*	*Share among Contestants (96)*	*Success Ratio (96)*
Andhra Pradesh	0.18	3.5	22.0
Arunachal Pradesh	0.07	2.4	46.7
Assam	0.14	2.3	22.4
Bihar	0.20	2.4	16.7
Goa	0.19	3.0	22.7
Gujarat	0.18	2.7	20.9
Haryana	0.36	2.8	17.3
Himachal Pradesh	0.17	3.1	21.7
Jammu & Kashmir	0.09	1.8	16.3
Karnataka	0.23	3.9	19.7
Kerala	0.13	2.7	27.5
Madhya Pradesh	0.20	3.0	25.2
Maharashtra	0.20	3.3	18.3
Manipur	0.08	1.4	2.9
Meghalaya	0.11	2.5	14.7
Mizoram	0.09	1.8	16.7
Nagaland	0.03	0.5	14.3
Orissa	0.16	2.8	25.9
Punjab	0.16	2.9	25.2
Rajasthan	0.20	2.7	24.6
Sikkim	0.28	4.8	8.3
Tamil Nadu	0.19	2.6	18.9
Tripura	0.13	3.0	22.7
Uttar Pradesh	0.28	2.6	14.8
West Bengal	0.12	2.6	27.8
Delhi	0.35	4.1	17.2
Pondicherry	0.18	3.7	14.3

In Bihar, the Congress till mid '70s played an important role in putting up women as candidates for Vidhan Sabha Elections and has returned the maximum number of women to Vidhan Sabha till 1985. In the 1985 elections out of the 13 who won eleven belonged to Congress I Party. This party had set up 32 candidates out of a total of 100 contestants. The Congress I has the record of setting up the largest number of women candidates for elections. Excepting in 1969 and 1977, 2/3 of the successful candidates have belonged to Congress I. Sumitra Devi, Uma Pandey won regularly from 1952 to 1967. Sumitra Devi won again in '69, and Ramdulari Sinha won, Uma Pandey and Ramdulari Sinha won again in 1972. In 70's and 80's Krishna Shahi, Prabhawati Gupta, Beula Doza, Manorama Pandey along with Uma Pandey repeated their success several times. Whenever things went bad for Congress Party, it had its repercussions on the election of women as in 1977 during the "Janata Wave", Congress Party once again came to limelight in 1985 with the Country-wide "sympathy wave" for Rajiv Gandhi and Congress I Party.

The SSP and PSP returned one or two candidates to Vidhan Sabha in first four elections. Parties like Jan Kranti Dal, Swatantra or Janata Party of Ramgarh house have had limited success Shashank Manjari won in the first four elections, changing party affiliations of one to other of these four parties.

In the late 50's and 60's, the non-Congress Parties which put up women candidates were Swatantra Party, Samyukta Socialist Party (SSP), Praja Socialist Party (SPS)[11] several independent women took their chance in 1971 and 1977 elections, but were routed. In 1977 Elections, the new Janata Party put up 10 women candidates for Vidhan Sabha elections, and all of the candidate's performed well by winning seats. As against Janata Party, Women candidates from Congress I could win only two seats.

The new Janata Dal came to power in 1990 with the slogan of establishing social equality and Justice in Bihar but this high ideal did not include women. In 1990 women were elected to Vidhan Sabha.[12] In 1995, 11 women could win the assembly elections. However, in the present Vidhan Sabha (2000) nineteen women are present.[13] Out of nineteen, seven won on BJP ticket. Veena Shahi has won on INC ticket, three women have won on SAP party. Sushila Hansda is from JMM Party and has moved to

Jharkhand. Joba Manjhi won on UGDP ticket and has gone to Jharkhand. Two women have won as Independent Candidates.

A review of the constituencies of these candidates reveals the fact that women MLAs have come from all corners of Bihar. Caste-wise women from Scheduled Castes and Backward Castes have had a fair representation in Vidhan Sabha.[14]

So far, in all 183 women have found entry into the Vidhan Sabha (See Appendix II). Many have come from good socio-economic background with political affiliations. The role of Patriarchy is still dominant in the planning of political careers of women in Bihar. Various election results have confirmed the political patronage enjoyed by some female candidates who have been successful several times. Uma Pandey who till 1989 has the record of six wins, had a Congress Leader as her father. Krishna Shahi is the daughter of Mahesh Prasad Sinha. Kishori Sinha is the wife of S.N. Sinha, while Prabhawati Singh is the daughter of Sir C.P.N. Singh. In the recent one decade a few women MLA have had political linkages before coming into the election fray. The State is being run now by Smt. Rabri Devi who has finally faced the electorate and won and is the wife of Laloo Prasad Yadav. Veena Shahi is the daughter-in-law of Congress old Stalwart Sri L.P. Shahi.

Literacy is not a single variable. It influences the number of contestants only in combination with other factors. The social 'ethos' and "taboos" prevailing in the State and in particular constituencies do influence the success or otherwise of the female contestants, but in a limited way. What matters most is the personality of the contestants including their family background and involvement in politics, local conditions, campaign strategy and the political party to which the candidates belong. Kamla Sinha was made Minister of State for External Affairs in the I.K. Gujral Cabinet during 1997-98.

Council of Ministers

The number of women from Bihar in the Union Cabinet and the State Council of Ministers has been very small. Yet women of Bihar have found a reasonable place in these bodies.

Union Cabinet— Women MP's in the earlier period of post-

Independence were well educated and some had brilliant academic careers. In the earlier Lok Sabha Tarkeshwari Sinha and Jahanara Jaipal Singh were quite well known. Tarkeshwari Sinha was the first women Deputy Finance Minister in the Nehru Ministry, Jahanara Jaipal Singh was nominated to Rajya Sabha in 1966 and held the portfolio of Transport and Civil Aviation. Ramdulari Sinha served as Minister of State in the Union Cabinet for two terms. She also held the post of Governor of Kerala for one year. Krishna Shahi was Minister of State in the 80's, Kanti Singh became State Minister for Coal in '96. In the present Cabinet ('99) Rita Verma is a Cabinet Minister.

State Level—Rani Jyotirmayee Devi was Deputy Minister for Welfare and Health along with Rajeshwari Saroj Das, Deputy Minister for Forest and Tribal Welfare in the Second Ministry from 6.5.57 to 31.1.61. Both of them were repeated as Deputy Minister in the third Ministry—18.2.61-14.2.62. In the fifth Ministry from 2.10.63 to 5.3.1967, Sumitra Devi became the first women Cabinet rank Minister for Information and Family Welfare, Premlata Rai became Cabinet Minister for P.H.E.D. and Family Welfare in the 6th Ministry in 1967. The 1972 Ministry had two Ministers—Sumitra Devi and Ramdulari Sinha of Cabinet rank. Beula Doza and Uma Pandey were Minister's of State. In 1977, Sumitra Devi was once again Cabinet Minister while Sushila Sahay and Kaushalya Devi were Ministers of State. In 1980, Prabhawati Gupta was State Minister for Jail while Uma Pandey was Minister of State for Tourism and Urban Development. In 1985 Uma Pandey became Cabinet Minister for Education, Rajbhasa, Science and Technology (Except Youth Welfare, Sports and Culture). Sushila Kerketta was State Minister for Irrigation. In 1988, Uma Pandey was Cabinet Minister for Revenue, Land Reforms and Stencila Hembram was State Minister for Health and Family Welfare. Sushila Kerketta was Cabinet Minister for Food and Civil Supply, Commerce, Rural Development while Sumitra Devi was made Cabinet Minister for Urban Development, Gayatri Devi became State Minister for Animal Husbandry and Fisheries. Ms Jyoti was made Deputy Minister for Education. Sumitra Devi, continued as Cabinet Minister, Urban Development between 6.12.89 to 10.3.90, but Uma Pandey was made Cabinet Minister for Human Resource Development and Rajbhasa. Sushila

Kerketta was made Cabinet Minister for Mines and Ms Jyoti became State Minister for Co-operative and Transport.

From March '90 to April '95. Sudha Srivastava was made Cabinet Minister for Health (except medical education) and Family Welfare. Shanti Devi was Deputy Minister for Transport. From April '95 to July '97 she was Cabinet Minister for Sugar Cane. Rabri Devi became Chief Minister on 25th July '97, and she had in her portfolio Cabinet Secretariat and Co-ordination, Home (excluding jail), Personnel Administration, Welfare, Civil Aviation. Shanti Devi became Cabinet Minister for Transport. Abo Devi was made State Minister for Rural Development and Sita Sinha was made State Minister for Welfare (excluding Tribal Welfare). In the 31st Ministry (8.3.99-3.3.2000) Rabri Devi continued as Chief Minister, and was in charge of Cabinet Secretariat and Co-ordination, Home (excluding Jail), Personnel Administration and Civil Aviation. Shanti Devi was Cabinet Minister for Transport. Abo Devi and Sita Sinha were State Minister. Abo Devi for Rural Development and Sita Sinha for Welfare (excluding Scheduled Caste).

In the present Ministry after General election 2000, Rabri Devi is the Chief Minister with the usual portfolios. Veena Shahi is Cabinet Minister for Co-operatives. She is from Congress I Party, Rama Devi is Cabinet Minister for PHED. Annapura Devi was State Minister for Mines and Minerals till 15.11.2000. Joba Manjhi was State Minister till 15.11.2000, i.e. creation of the separate Jharkhand State (See Appendix-III).

A perusal of women's political activities in Bihar makes it very clear that women of this State are scarce in National as well as State Politics. They have not been mobilized property even as voters in both, Lok Sabha and Vidhan Sabha Elections. In Lok Sabha Elections, the maximum mobilization of women voters from Bihar has been 55.83 per cent in 1998. Bihar has been one of the five lowest mobiliser States of women voters for Lok Sabha Elections. In Bihar Vidhan Sabha Elections, the maximum mobilization of women has been 42.58 per cent in 1995 elections. Otherwise, it has averaged between 30 per cent to 40 per cent in all elections. Similarly, their membership in Lok Sabha and Bihar Vidhan Sabha has been very small. In Bihar Vidhan Sabha, the maximum has been 10.49 per cent in 1957. After '62, the percentage has averaged between 3 per cent to 4 per cent with the exception of 2000 Elections. At present nineteen women (5.86 per cent) are in the Bihar Vidhan Sabha. Same is the case with Bihar Vidhan Parishad.

Therefore, the urgency of investigation into the low political participation of women of Bihar needs hardly be over emphasized. It is necessary to find why women in Bihar have not become viable as "political actors" in Bihar. The fact that Bihar is being ruled by a women Chief Minister for the last three and a half years, is hardly significant. It is an 'open' truth that Bihar is still ruled by Laloo Prasad Yadav, and installation of Rabri Devi as Chief Minister is in reality a 'slap' to the feminist movements, women's movements. It is yet another feather in the crown of everlasting and ever-important "Patriarchy".

Thus this topic has been taken for investigation and analysis. Studies on Women in the local regional context of Bihar are scarce in general and very very non-existent in the area of politics-or political participation. The following chapter will give a glimpse of the methodology used for this study/ investigation.

REFERENCES

1. Elina, Havio Manila *et al.*,—*Unfinished Democracy.* Oxford, Pergamon 1983.
2. Kumari Abhilasha and Kidwai Sabina—*Crossing the Sacred Line: Women in search for Political Power*—Published by Fredrick Ebert Stiftung, New Delhi-49, Introduction, pp. 3-4.
3. *Ibid.*
4. Sapiro, Virginia—*What research on Political Socialisation tells us:* p. 163. Carol Palewan Women and Political Issue in Politics, Vol. 17, No. 1, p. 45.
5. Paper of UNICEF, PATNA.
6. *Sadasya Soochi — Bihar Vidhan Sabha,* Bihar Government Publication 1075.
7. *Bihar Vidhan Sabha Ke Sadasyon Ka Sanchipta Jeevan Parichay*—Feb. 1966, Bihar Vidhan Sabha, p. 114.
8. *General Elections to Bihar Legislative Assembly: Statistical Analysis* 1977, 1980.
9. *General Elections to Bihar Vidhan Sabha 1985: A Statistical Analysis,* Secretariat Press, Patna 1086.

10. Sharan Sarojini—The Role of Women in Bihar General Elections (1967) in the Report "As Study of the 4th General Elections in Bihar 1967". Published by the Institute of Public Administration, Patna University, pp. 253-254.
11. *Ibid.*, p. 255.
12. *The Hindustan Times.* Patna (daily newspaper) Monday March 5, 1990, p. 4.
13. General Elections to Bihar Vidhan Sabha—1995, 2000. Statistical Analysis.
14. *Op cit.,* Report of the 4th General Elections, Bihar.

2
Methodology

Formulation of the Problem

Bihar is regarded as one of the most backward States of the Indian Union. It is not backward only on economic front. It suffers from social backwardness also which is reflected very sharply in the status of women in Bihar. The Development index points towards the poverty, illiteracy and very low social status of women. They are marginalized in all spheres of life and especially so in politics. Their participation in structural politics is very low. For decades Bihar has been one of the five lowest mobiliser States of women voters. So women in Bihar have not been mobilized even as voters. The political parties do not put up a reasonable number of women candidates, so women in Bihar suffer from rigid social structures on the one hand, low life conditions and apathy from political parties and political leadership on the other hand. Women hardly get access to the decision-making structures and processes. Why is it so? The study has been undertaken with the following objectives:-

Objectives of the Study

The main focus of the study is participation of women in structural politics. As discussed earlier, their participation is very low and the picture is gloomy. It is necessary to find out the bottlenecks that prevent the political participation of women in a meaningful manner, and hence obstruct their empowerment. The main objectives of the study are as follows:

1. To asses the participation of women as voters in elections.
2. To asses the candidature of women for various elections.

3. To asses the factors responsible for their defeat in elections.
4. To asses the role of women as decision makers in the capacity of member of Lok Sabha, State Assemblies, Union Cabinet and State Council of Minister.
5. To identify the various obstacles in the path of women's political empowerment.

Hypothesis

Following hypothesis have been taken into account which have been tested in this study:

1. Is political participation of women overshadowed by "Gender Consideration"?
2. Does "Patriarchy" prevent women's access to political institutions and processes?
3. Does the socio-economic and cultural environment of women determine women's level of political participation?
4. Does the culture of violence in politics affect women's participation in politics?
5. Does lack of aptitude and awareness of politics affect women's political participation?

Method of Study

The study is an "Empirical Study" of women in structural politics in Bihar. The method of Social Survey has been applied. Among the various methods in social survey, sample survey method has been adopted. Apart from this, participatory and case-study methods have also been used marginally Through participative method it was possible to have some in-depth information, which enriched the date-analysis. Through case-study method it was possible to acquire a deep insight into the political participation of some of the noted "political women" in Bihar.

Universe of the Study

The Universe of the study is the State of Bihar. Effort has

been made to cover most of the geographical regions of Bihar.

Sample

The Random Sampling and Quota Sampling methods have been used in this study for various categories of respondents. The sample consists of 350 respondents categorized in the following manner:

(A) Women Voters-200. Maximum respondents belong to this category because "Voting" is the most "Common" political activity performed by the largest number of citizens. It is the 'life-breath' of Indirect Democracy. Random Sampling method has been used to select respondents in this category.

(B) Women Political Activities-50. The respondents have been taken from different political parties. Quota sampling method has been used for selecting this category of respondents.

(C) Women Contestants who 'lost' elections (never won) 50. The method used for selecting respondents in this category is Quota Sampling. Respondents have been selected from the list of contestants who never did win any election.

(D) Elected and held positions in Lok Sabha Vidhan Sabha's and Union Cabinet and Council of Ministers — 50. The method of quota sampling has been used to select respondents in this category, so as to cover persons from the first Lok Sabha/Bihar Vidhan Sabha and Cabinet and Council of Ministers to the present.

Data Collection and Analysis

(A) Some Data has been collected through Secondary Sources—

Books, Reports, Journals and newspapers, especially for Introduction and Profile of Bihar.

(B) Data through structured schedule has been collected from the selected 350 respondents from structural political bodies. In-depth interview of a few selected women leaders have been taken, and also some case-histories of very 'dynamic' political women leaders have been prepared to gain more 'insight' into the matter.

The Schedule is divided into four following sections:

(A) Socio-economic and educational background.

(B) Self Perception of women.

(C) Part 'C' has two sub-sections.

- (a) Political Aptitude,
- (b) Political Awareness.

(D) Political participation of women. It has three sub-sections

- (a) Political activities—this section contains questions for women who have held positions in political structures as legislators and decision-makers.
- (b) Voting, contesting elections.
- (c) Desire to contest Elections, and opinion on important current political issues.

Data Analysis

Data was put into Tabler Form with percentage for scientific analysis for final inferences. Data has been coded and analysed manually with the help a professional data analyst.

Significance of the Study

The significance of the study can hardly be over-estimated. Political participation by women who constitute nearly 50 per cent of the total population is necessary for the healthy working of a Democratic Polity which is supposed to be a rule by the people for the people, and of the people. Surety women constitute 50 per cent of the "People".

India is a vast country, with multi-layered regional, cultural religious, lingual and level of economic development variations. These factors to a great extent affect individual behaviour. Same is the case with women. Their marginal political participation and/ or apathy towards politics has to be understood in the context of these variations. Hence, the need for an study of women's political participation in regional-local context. This will also help identify the factors which create hurdles in the way of meaningful participation by women in politics, which can finally ensure their empowerment.

Thus, this study has been undertaken within the geographical and socio-economic and cultural boundary of one State — Bihar. Bihar has played an important role in National Politics as well with 54 seats in Lok Sabha until the creation of Jharkhand State on 15th November, 2000. Further, Bihar has been in the forefront in challenging the hegemony of political power wielded by Congress Party at the Centre from 1967 onwards. The Total Revolution led by Jai Prakash Narain in 1974 shook the very foundation of Indira Gandhi's government and finally led to the massive defeat of the Congress Party in 1977. Bihar which stands very low in the Development Index, nevertheless has been playing a very crucial role in National Politics. The Women from Bihar though small in number have fared well in Lok Sabha and their presence in Bihar Vidhan Sabha is not too bad. Therefore, this study has been undertaken to map out a true picture of women's political participation in Bihar, to identify the factors which have prevented Bihari women from playing a more meaningful role both in the State and at the Centre. Strategies will be planned on the basis of available information to increase the participation of women in political structures and processes. This will lead the way for the empowerment of women of Bihar. The study is a significant effort because not much has been written on women and politics in Bihar, and there is a serious lack of information about women's political activities in Bihar.

3

Profile of Bihar: The Situational Context

The State of Bihar came into existence on March 22, 1912, as a response to the Declaration of "Delhi Durbar' is 1911. Orissa which was with Bihar became a separate State in 1936. Till recently Bihar has been the second most populous State of India. On 15.11.2000, a new State carved out of Bihar, the Jharkhand State came into existence with a population of nearly 2.80 crores. Eighty-one seats out of the 324 Bihar Vidhan Sabha seats have gone to Jharkhand State. Out of the earlier 54 seats which Bihar had in Lok Sabha fourteen have gone to Jharkhand.[1] Eighteen MLA's and sixteen ministers were withdrawn from the Rabri Devi Ministry from the midnight of 15.11 2000[2]. However, the scope of this study covers the undivided Bihar as far as empirical investigations are concerned. A short profile of Bihar is given below to understand the situational context in which the respondents have participated in politics.

Demography

The State has a population density of 880. The density is very high in North Bihar Plains, almost the highest in India. The density of population in Central Bihar is equally high, but it is more development and urbanized. The plateau region of Chotanagpur and Santhal Parganas which now form the new State of Jharkhand is remarkably different from these two regions. The decaded growth in the State population for the decade 1991-2001 is 28.43 per cent. The total population of Bihar is 8,28,787.96 including 43153964 males and 39724832 females as per 2001 Census of Bihar. The growth of population in the composite Bihar had been lower than the national average but between

1991-2001 it has increased roughly by 5 per cent being at 28.4 per cent as against 21.34 per cent in India. Bihar now consists of 8.07 per cent of the total population of the country (Table 1).

TABLE 1

Decennial Growth of Population in Bihar 1901-2001

The Gender Composition

Year	*Total Population*	*Male*	*Female*	*All India Average*
1901	27,311,865	13,294,266	14,01,599	238,396,327
1911	26,314,281	13,854,679	14,549,602	252,093,399
1921	28,926,675	13,954,010	14,172,665	251,321,213
1931	31,347,108	15,724,504	15,622,605	278,977,238
1941	35,170,840	17,622,539	17,548,301	318,660,580
1951	38,782,271	19,489,964	19,292,307	361,088,090
1961	46,497,457	23,301,449	23,154,161	439,234,771
1971	56,354,369	28,846,944	27,506,425	548,150,652
1981	69,823,154	35,865,467	33,957,687	683,329,097
1991	86,338,853	45,147,280	41,191,573	
2001	82,878,796	43,153,964	39,724,832	

Source: 1. Census of India 1971 General Population Tables (1901-1951) Services and Services, Part IIA(i), New Delhi, Registrar General and Census Commission, 1975, p. 131.

2. Census Reports—1961, 71, 81, 91 (1961-1991) Office of the Registrar General of India, Ministry of Home Affairs.

3. Provisional Statistics revealed by Director of Census Operations in Bihar on 26.3.2001.

Sex-ratio— A disturbing demographic indictor has been one of declining sex-ratio in the State. It is more distressing because it is the same State where women outnumbered men as per 1921 Census when the ratio was 1016 females to 1000 males. However, the situation looks slightly improved as per the disclosures of the Director of Census operations, Bihar on March 26, 2001. The present sex-ratio is 921 females per 1000 males. It has registered an upward trend in almost all the districts of Bihar. The sole exception is Bhojpur district where the sex-ratio has declined slightly and Vaishali where it has remained unchanged (Table 2).

TABLE 2

Sex Ratio in Bihar 1901-2001

Year	*BIHAR*		*INDIA*	
	Male	*Female*	*Male*	*Female*
1921	1000	1016	1000	955
1931	1000	994	1000	950
1941	1000	996	1000	945
1951	1000	990	1000	946
1961	1000	994	1000	941
1971	1000	956	1000	930
1081	1000	946	1000	934
1991	1000	912	1000	927
2001*	1000	921	1000	933

Source: Culled from Census of India Reports, Office of the Registrar General of India, Ministry of Home Affairs.

Source: Census of India 1971, General Publication Table Govt. of India, Part II (A); New Delhi Registrar General and Census Commission, 1975, p. 126.

* Data given by the Director of Census Operations, Bihar on 26.3.2001 and quoted in *Hindustan Times* (Daily Newspaper) Patna dated 27.3.2001, p. 1.

As per a recent report of UNICEF, Patna, more than 8 lakh girls in the age-group of 10-14 years in Bihar are missing. The sex-ratio in this age-groups is 834 girls per 1000 boys. UNICEF Patna reports that female infanticide is still in practice in some regions of the State and 16 lakh more girls would have been alive in Bihar today.

Infant Mortality Rate— The infant mortality ratio of children of Bihar was 124 girls in per 1000 live births in 1981, and 71 per 1000 live births in 1991. The situation is showing some signs of improvement as seen in Table 3.

TABLE 3

INFANT MORTALITY RATE—BIHAR

(Per Thousand Live Births)

Year	*Male*	*Female*
1981	112	124
1991	68	71

Source: National Institute of Public Co-operation and Child Development: Statistics on Children in India Pocket Berra 1997, New Delhi, NIPCCD, 1997, p. 53.

Marriage— The Singular mean age at marriage of girls in Bihar is 18 (Table 4). Age specific fertility rate of girls who are 19 or less is 65.5. Only four States in India have a higher fertility rate—Andhra Pradesh, Madhya Pradesh, Rajasthan and West Bengal (UNICEF Report). The maternal death per 100,000 births are 4709.

TABLE 4

Singular Mean Age of Marriage in Bihar

Year	*Male*	*Female*	*Difference*
1961	18.9	14.3	4.6
1971	20.0	16.6	4.7
1981	21.6	16.6	5.0
1993	23.2	18.0	5.2

Source: Population Research Centre, Patna University International Institute for Population Science, Bombay.

National Family Health Survey 1993 International Institute for Population Science, 1995, p. 55.

Economy

The economy of Bihar is predominantly agriculture based and rural. The ratio of urbanization is 13.17 per cent as against the national average of 25.72 per cent in 1991.[4] 86.83 per cent of the total population in Bihar lives in rural areas. Almost 79 per cent of the population is directly or indirectly dependent on agriculture for livelihood. It has 115 lakh ha cultivated land out of a total of 174 lakh ha. However only 85 lakh hectares of land is cultivated currently. However, Bihar presents a paradox of poor agricultural performance amidst plenty of rich river streams, high fertility of soil of the Gangetic plain and hard working labour resources. This state of affairs is also directly related to the slow rate or industrial development. The State continues to be deficit in food grain production despite 90.3 per cent area under food-grains production. The result is very low yield of food grains. Irrigation is poor and irrigated land is just 38.2 per cent as compared to 92 per cent in Punjab and 67.1 per cent in Haryana. The situation with regard to other technological inputs is equally discouraging. The perils of frequent floods in North Bihar area repeated every year. Recurrence of embankment failures have assumed unmanageable proportions.

The agrarian structure is outmoded. Absentee land-ownership, large and scattered holdings, insecure tenancies, fragmented holdings and iniquitous agrarian relations are constraints to rapid agricultural growth and economic development. Land reforms have been enacted but they have not been implemented properly. The measures of reform that could have benefited the disadvantaged groups of marginal peasants, share-croppers and landless labourers are enforcement of ceiling on agricultural holdings and the redistribution of homestead tenancies. Half hearted efforts and slip-shod manner of execution has resulted in the redistribution of only about one per cent of the available land in the State.[5]

The poor performance of Bihar in land reform implementation is rooted primarily in the very structure of rural power relations and caste alliances at the village level. Large landowners are not only economically affluent but socially protent and politically powerful. The existing legal system leans favourably towards the rich and the influential.

Poverty—The successive NSS rounds indicate that the absolute number of the poor is estimated to have grown by 33 per cent between the early seventies and the late eighties. As many as 77 per cent of farm labourers and 47 per cent of the persons in farm households with land of their own are below the poverty line. The extent of unemployment in Bihar stands at 2.84 per cent (usual Principal Status) of labour force.

According to the data released in 1987-88. 42.7 per cent of the total rural population lives below the poverty line.[6] As per 1997-1998 Reports, 56 per cent of the population lives below poverty line in Bihar.[7]

Level of Urbanization in Bihar is very low. As per 1991 Census it is just 13.17 per cent as against the national average of 25.79 per cent as can be seen from Table 5.

TABLE 5

Level of Urbanization in Bihar 1951-1991
Urban Population 5 Per Cent of Total Population

Year	*% of Urban Population to Total Population*
1951	6.8
1961	8.4
1971	10.0
1981	12.5
1991	13.17
2001	13.17

Source: (i) Centre of Monitoring Indian Economic. Basic Statistics relating to Indian Economic, Vol. 2 States. Sept. 1988, Bombay, 1988.

(ii) Census of India, 1991, Series 1 India, paper II of 1991 Provisional Publication totals; Rural-Urban distribution, New Delhi Registrar General & Census Commissioner, 1991, p. 16.

TABLE 6

Work Participation of Women in Bihar—Main and Marginal
Year 1981-1991

		1981	*1991*
Main Workers	Total	20712215	25652569
	Male	17603355	21342198
	Female	3108860	4310371
Marginal Workers	Total	1792981	2459027
	Male	365591	307520
	Female	1427390	2151507
% of Main Workers to total Population	Total	29.66	29.71
	Male	40.08	47.47
	Female	9.16	10.27

Work Participation— As per '91 Census the work participation ratio of women in just 14.86 per cent as against the males 47.92 per cent (Table 6).

The total percentage of female main workers to total population is just 10.27. In the Agriculture sector, there are 57.92 per cent women as labourers while 31.57 per cent only are cultivators. In the Industry Sector only 2.86 per cent are in household industries, and 7.68 per cent women are in other services (Table 7) (Detailed Table in Appendix-I).

TABLE 7

Distribution of Female Workers by Broad Agricultural and Industrial Categories Work Participation of Women in Bihar 1971-1991

Year	*Total Female Population*	*Total no of*	*Agriculture*		*Industry*	
		Female main worker	*Cultivator*	*Agriculture Labourers*	*House-holds Industry*	*Other services*
1951						
1961						
1971	2516009	114330	5279	30258		
			(17.35%)	(73.61)	(2.44%)	(6.60%)
1981	33957689	3108860	79895	1944282	102359	263324
			(25.70%)	(62.54)	(3.29%)	(8.47%)
1991	81191573	4310371	1352408	2496393	123350	331230
			(31.57%)	(57.92%)	(2.86%)	(7.68%)

Sources: Census Reports 1981,1991, Series 4 of the Reports.

The trends in work participation rate by gender from 1911-1991, shows that women's participation rate has been going down since 1931 with one exception of 1961 (Table 8).

According to NSS organization survey of July, 1993, in every 1000 there are just 155 women who are engaged in some sort of work.

TABLE 8

Trends in Work Participation Rate by Gender in Bihar 1911-1991

Year	*Person*	*Male*	*Female*
1911	48.42	62.52	34.71
1921	49.52	63.31	35.94
1931	41.45	56.71	26.09
1951	35.80	50.70	2.75
1961	41.46	55.71	27.13
1971	41.51	52.51	9.80
1981	32.35	50.18	13.50
1991	32.16	47.92	14.86

Source: Census of India, Occassional paper No. 8 of 1988, Analysis of work force, New Delhi, Manager of Publication, 1989, p. 54.

Agrawal, A.N. and Verma, Hariom Indian Economy: Statistical Year Book, 1998, New Delhi, National Publishing House, 1998, p. 84.

Education— The literacy ratio of Bihar has always been very low. From 34 million illiterates in 1951 it increased to 58 million in 1991. In 1991 the total literate's percentage was 38.54 out of which the percentage of female literates was just 23.19 per cent as compared to the males 52.63 per cent. However, the decade 1991-2001 shows some favourable signs. As per the data released by the Director of Census Operations Bihar on 26.3.2001, the total literacy rate in Bihar is now 47.53 per cent. However, out of the total literates 60.32 per cent are males while the percentage of literate women in Bihar is still just 33.57. As against the national average of 65.38, Bihar's literacy growth is still very slow, especially women's literacy. Their literacy percentage falls much below the national average of literacy for women which is 54.16 per cent.

District-wise female literacy rate is highest in Patna district (52.17), followed by Munger (47.97). It is lowest still in Kishanganj district (18.49), followed by Supaul (21.02) and Araria (22.31) (Table 9 & 10).

TABLE 9

Literacy by Gender in Bihar-1951-2001

Year	*Total*	*Male*	*Female*
1951	12.2	20.5	3.8
1961	21.8	35.2	8.2
1921	19.94	30.64	8.72
1981	26.20	38.11	13.62
1991	39.00	53.00	23.00
1995	4.00	59.00	28.00
1997	49.00	62.00	34.00
2001*	47.53	60.22	33.57

Source: 1. Literacy Rate has been counted for 7 + years from 1981 & onwards.

2. Census of India 1981 series I India Part II B (i) Primary Census Abstract General Population, New Delhi, Registrar General & Census Commission 1986, p. 17.

Central Statistical Organisation, Statistical Abstract of India 1998, New Delhi, Manager of Publications, 1999, pp. 483-489.

3. Provisional data released by Director of Census operations, Bihar on March 26, 2001 quoted in *Hindustan Times*, Patna (Daily newspaper) dated 27.3.2001.

TABLE 10

District-wise Female Literacy Rate in Bihar: 2001

	Highest Female Literacy		*Lowest Female Literacy*	
District	Patna district	(51.17)	Kishanganj	(18.49)
	Munger district	(47.97)	Supaul	(21.02)
	Rohtas district	(46.92)	Madhepura	(22.31)

Source: Provisional data released by Director of Census Operations Bihar on 26.3.2001 and quoted by *Hindustan Times*, Patna (daily newspaper) dated 27.3.2001.

The drop-out ratio of girls in Classes I-V was 68.93 per cent as against boys 63.88 per cent in 1987-88 (Table 11).

TABLE 11

Drop-out Rates at Primary Education Leveling Bihar by Gender Class I-V Year 1977-1988

Year	*Total*	*Male*	*Female*
1977-78	65.7	64.0	70.3
1978-79	49.2	46.6	52.9
1979-80	52.1	50.5	54.4
1980-81	55.3	53.5	58.0
1981-82	54.6	53.2	56.7
1988-89	65.63	63.88	68.93

Source: Centre for Monitoring Indian Economy: Basic Statistics relating to Indian Economic, Vol. II, Sept. 1992, Bombay, CMIE, p. 1-14.

The socio-economic and educational profile of Bihar presents a grim picture. The challenges of solving poverty, illiteracy, unemployment, primary health and nutrition problems are momentous. It is still more pathetic when we come to the life-conditions of women in Bihar. A good administration under the premiership of a thoughtful, humane and dynamic political leader could achieve the 'rebirth' of Bihar, what one witnesses today is a total collapse of administrative machinery in Bihar. The social structure in Bihar is still predominantly feudal, and the persistence of feudal values and the resultant conflicts are amply visible especially in the rural areas. Land ownership is still in the hands of the rich upper and intermediary castes, who have joined hands in an effort to continue the "old order" with a vengeance. Land reforms have not been implemented and minimum wages for agricultural labour are still not operational in most of the rural areas in Bihar. The 'labourers' the dalits are still regarded as "serfs" and whenever there is a resistance to this order, bloody caste/class wars between the two parties takes place.

Caste—Caste is indeed a force to be reckoned with, throughout India. It controls all social, economic and political relationships of the individuals and is everywhere the unit of social action.[8]

Caste, is the most important characteristics of the social system in Bihar and has always influenced politics as well. During the 50's and 60's politics of Bihar was dominated by upper castes under the rule of Congress Party. Voters were mobilized, tickets for election were distributed on caste lines. Even ministries were allocated on caste preferences. It has continued and continued with a vengeance. Political developments, particularly in Bihar are nucleating around the caste-system for wishful gain by the elite of the different caste-strata for clinching the political power on the basis of caste groups. After the 1967 General Elections, Bihar saw an experiment in unstable coalition governments, ridden with caste-loyalties and political factionalism. The political mobilization of the lower middle and lower castes started and they aspired for the opportunity to have a share in the political structures. The 'Reservation' issue raised by the Janata government during 1977 helped this sentiment to develop.[9] Since 1989 this caste factor took a serious turn and the 'Backward' caste entered the portals of Bihar Politics under the leadership of Laloo Prasad Yadav in 1990. For the last eleven years, politics in Bihar is totally directed by caste considerations. To be precise, it is not even "backward castes' now—it is the rule of one caste—'the Yadavas'. Persistence of Feudal values and caste polarization into Forward Castes and Backward Castes has disrupted normal life in Bihar—its economy, education, development has reached the level of a 'Big Zero'. A total culture of violence operates in Bihar.

The Culture of Violence in Bihar

Extremism and cult of violence is prevailing in Bihar persistently since the last quarter of the Century. Violent conflicts and mass scale massacres are now common incidents due to various social and economic reasons. We have the Feudal machinery at work by the big and high caste landlords on the one hand and the popular movements, the Naxal movements of the socially and economically weak, the poor and the Dalit on the other hand waging blood wars with each other. Nearly 41 districts from the 54 of the erstwhile Bihar are extremism infected areas with various extremist political group gaining ground everyday. Starting from Belchi in 1979 where 11 dalits were mercilessly massacred and which later became a political issue. Bihar has to date witnessed almost seventy massacres since 1977 in which either dalits have been murdered or some high caste groups have been killed. The worst slaughter of Harijans by the

Ranveer Sena on the night of December 1, 1997 around 9.30 P.M. in the villages of Bathani Tola, part of Laxmanpur Bathe in Jehanabad District stunned the nation. As Bathani Tola went to sleep that night, no one knew that 61 villagers—35 women and 19 children would never see the light of December 2. They became victims of the worst carnage in Bihar's violent history—mercilessly gunned down by the Ranveer Sena.[10] (See list in Appendix).

The most prominent organized caste and class groups are the upper castes/ Bhumihar with their Ranveer Sena on the one hand, the poor and Dalit Communities organized by leftist groups such as M.C.C., P.W.G., C.P.I. (ML). Keeping personal armies by rich landlords and big cultivators is nothing new in Bihar such as Bhoomi Sena, Lorik Sena, Sunlight Sena etc. in the 70's and the early massacres in Belchi, Pipra, Rupaspur etc. But since the 90's it has assumed vast proportions with the emergence of Ranveer Sena of the Bhumihars and more and more mobilization of Dalits by the left groups. It is a direct confrontation with most polished and new ultra-modern weapons killing in large numbers.

Ghosh remarks— The Police force is poorly equipped and staffed. While the don's fight among themselves with their LMGs and SLRs, the Police use World War II weapons and wireless sets. The population—Police ratio is perhaps the lowest in the country. Worst, at the Thana level, caste influences postings. Nearly 80 percent of the SHOs in charge of Police stations are Yadavas, belonging to Chief Ministers Caste.[11] Villages have been turned into barren fields. The year '99 was one such year when the in-famous massacres of Senari, Shankerpur etc. took place. In all these massacres women are a major target. The Ranveer Sena targeted even pregnant women with bullets exclaiming that they will not allow future Naxals to be born. The data reveals that with the emergence of Ranveer Sena the killings have intensified to great proportion. From March 1990 to March '95, 11 massacres had taken place due to Ranveer Sena initiative but it increased to 37 between 1995-2000. The number of peoples killed in massacres before Ranveer Sena from 1990-94 had been 108 which later increased to 367.[12] The rural population in Central Bihar villages lives in an environment of suspended animation—awaiting killings any moment. Women have been left alone without any means of livelihood. All activities are almost suspended.

Criminalisation of Politics

In Bihar, criminalisation of politics has become a cliche today. By the 70's politics in the country was in the deep forays of crime The 70's were a period of turbulent events in Bihar. On the one hand, a strong movement against corruption of the Government was taking root and spreading in Bihar under the leadership of Jai Prakash Narain in 1974, on the other hand the Government at the Centre was finding its roots shaking. With the declaration of Emergency on June 25, 1975 was started in earnest a process of repression of political opponents. The Congress was routed in 77 Election, and Janata Party Governments were established at the centre and in the States, Bihar being one such State. However, negative trends developed very soon, and the management of the movement fell in the hands of lumpen elements. This was the time when Laloo Prasad Yadav emerged on the political scene winning Lok Sabha Election from Chapra. It was in 1977 that the seeds of future politics in Bihar were sown. Bihar suffered from governmental instability during the Janata rule of Karpoori Thakur. The Congress came back to power in 1980, and the 1980's can well be described as the decade of the "Criminal politicians". One murder that shook Begusarai was that of the Communist stalwart Indradev Singh on 18th September, 1983. Frequent murders of political leaders, and changes in the Chief Ministership of the State happened. On 10th March, 1990 Laloo Prasad Yadav took oath of office. From that day onward there was naked vulgarisation of political life in Bihar.[13] The decade of 90's opened with a bang for political criminals. The murder of Congress MLA Hemant Shahi in March '99 sent shockwaves throughout the State. The second term of Laloo Prasad Yadav as Chief Minister has been a witness to gruesome political killings. The Parliamentary elections of 1991 had been one of the most violent in Bihar with a lot of blood shedding. Similarly the State Assembly elections of 1995 saw a series of murders.[14] The story of violent and Criminal Politics is continuing in the rule of Rabri Devi, the present Chief Minister. Undoubtedly, the flag of arbitrariness in Bihar has been flying higher and higher. Nobody has control over political crimes.[15] Mindless killings directly or indirectly are related to and are results of this sort of politics.

The political structures have become the shelter grounds for openly declared, charge sheeted criminals. In the one decade of JD/RJD rule Bihar has become a sick state plagued with Caste-Violence amounting to mass-scale killings, abductions, women specific crimes. The 2000 elections witnessed the open induction of criminals into politics by giving them party-tickets for elections. Some fought from behind bars and even won. In the present Vidhan Sabha and Council of Ministers, there is no dearth of criminals present. You look for one and find many easily. (See list in Appendix).

Violence against Women

The lives of women have been affected very badly in this culture of violence. Due to the utter collapse of administration and total erosion of Civic Values women are neither safe at home nor outside or in their work-place. There has been a very sharp increase in crimes against women especially since the Janata Dal Government was installed under the premiership of Laloo Prasad Yadav a decade ago. A leader who had ten years ago pledged to bring social equality and justice in Bihar has been directly or indirectly responsible for the collapse of law and order, increased support to induction of criminals openly in the Government. Caste wars, gang-wars, abductions and women specific crimes such as rape, torture, abduction, killing of women in caste gang-wars are the order of the day. After his forced exit from power, his wife Smt. Rabri Devi became the Chief Minister of Bihar on July 25, 1997. Let us take a glance at what has happened in the last three and a half years to women under the rule of a woman Chief Minister.

The Chart Below Gives an Oveview of Crimes against Women from 1997

Year	*Rape*	*Abduction*	*Eve-teasing*	*Dowy death*	*Torture*
1997	1318	336	178	420	233
1998	1305	394	181	531	974
1999	1139	433	427	350	955

Sources: Crime Investigation Department, Bihar.

The data till '98 September reveals that young girls, minor girls of different communities have not been safe in the regime of a women Chief Minister in Bihar:

Rape of minor girls	1764
Rape of Tribal girls	652
Rape of Scheduled Castes girls	1264
Rape of women from higher caste communities	3534
Eve-teasing and torture	3266
Dowry deaths	1923
Rape and murder (Total)	3843

In caste massacres women have been made special targets. In caste massacres in Bathani Tolaon 10.7.96, Ekwari 10.4.97, Bathe 31.12.97, Shankar Bigha January '99, Narayanpur 10.2.99, there were cases of pegnant women being specifically killed, while the killers screaming that '"no-naxal" will be allowed to be born'. From April 1995 to June 2000, 37 massacres have happened in Bihar and it is 3.37 per cent more than what happened earlier. The whole of Central Bihar is in the grip of caste violence, massacres, the economy being totally destroyed with villages wearing a deserted look.

Thus, this is the present scenario in Bihar. On the one hand there are the feudal forces aggressively at work disrupting the socio-economic and political structures, on the other hand there is a tremendous growth of populist movements especially in the Central Bihar regions. Extremist left outfits are growing and spreading rapidly, mobilizing the 'dalits'—the have-not's. The result is a continuous chain of gang-wars and massacres between the rich landlords/upper caste and the poor/down-trodden. The CPI ML picked up Bihar as an area of its operations because it felt that the rural Bihar was steeped in Feudal practices—the nexus of upper caste/Intermediary Caste land owners, the administration and political leaders ruthlessly repressing the poor low-castes peasants. In various area these poor dalits have been strongly mobilized for fighting the upper caste landowners. Neither party is ready to back out. The result is unabated violence in the form of mass-massacres, killings. There is the "Ranveer Sena" of the rich and high-caste landowners and there are the group organized by P.W.G. (People's war group) M.C.C. and CPI ML.

Thus two totally contradictory forces are juxtaposed against each other in Bihar—the 'Feudal' and the 'Populist' or 'Liberationist' forces. In their bloody struggle and confrontations, the development and progress of Bihar has taken a back-seat. There is utter lawlessness and anarchy prevailing in Bihar.

Women in Bihar are living in such an environment of violence, crime, and total collapse of law and order. Their poverty, illiteracy and an environment of contained violence can hardly be conductive to their meaningful participation in socio-political life. It is a viscious circle; for eradicating poverty and illiteracy, some sort of order and development is the necessary precondition. Above all they need protection of their lives and their work. If the Government of the day is not able to put a stop to this mad run for power by the various castes, continuance of feudal practices, and work for providing better opportunities for education, health and jobs, women in Bihar will not be able to create 'space' for themselves in the arena of politics.

Women's political participation has to be understood in the situational context of the environment in Bihar.

REFERENCES

1. The Times of India, Patna (Daily Newspaper) 15.11.2000, p. 1.
2. *The Indian Nation*, Patna (Daily Newspaper) August 14, 2000—MLA's in Jharkhand Proposed State.
3. (a) Reports of Census of India.
   (b) Provisional data released by the Director of Census Operations Bihar on 26.3.2001.
4. Karna, M.N.—*Bihar: A Profile*—A.N. Sinha Institute of Social Studies, Patna Report of the "Hunger Project" March, 1994.
5. *Ibid.*
6. Authorised data released in 1987-88 Based on evaluation of monetary income by Planning Commission, India.
7. Based on the "Specialists' Team" Report 1995 of Planning Commission, India.
8. Mitra, Roma — *Caste Polarization and politics* published by Syndicate Publishers (India), Ashok Rajpath-1992, Introduction, p. 1.
9. *Ibid.*, pp. 2 & 3.

10. Ghosh S.K.—*Bihar in Flames.* A.P.H. Publishing Corporation, 5, Ansari Road, Daryaganj, New Delhi-2, quoted by K.F. Rustamji in the Forward p. VIII.
11. *Ibid.*
12. *Ye Jang Jaroor Jeetewge*—Published by CPI ML, Patna, 7, Patel Road, Patna-1, p. 33.
13. Jha, Vikas Kumar—*Bihar: Rajniti Ka Apradhikaran* (in Hindi), translated in English by Ms Ruby Roy and named—"Bihar: Criminalisation of Politics," Shristi Prakashan, Patna-800 001, 1996, pp. 32-40.
14. *Ibid.*, pp. 87-88.
15. *Ibid.*, p. 99.

4

Women as Voters

Of the various activities termed as "Political", voting is the most common activity performed by citizens in large numbers in a Democratic set up of government. Although voting percentage does not go beyond 50 even in the most classical example of Democracy, that is U.S.A. This is the activity in which most of the citizens participate. It is a very important activity because through voting people decide the type of governance they want and choose their representatives for governance. Through voting the people provide legitimacy to the authority and urge them to be responsible to the people. Indirect Democracy, the most prevalent form of Democracy can be run only when the citizens vote and vote properly.

Women in Bihar have not been mobilized even as voters by the political parties for long. Bihar has persistently been one of the five states with lowest mobilization of women as voters. However, there has been considerable increase in the percentage of women voters in the last one and a half decades. The manner in which they vote is a matter which needs a separate debate considering the low indicators of women's literacy, poverty.

To analyze the role of women voters in Bihar, this category of respondents includes the largest number 200—in our sample. While respondent in other categories also have been and are voters, this category exclusively contains respondents who have not participated or been associated with any other political activity ever, except voting. It is a mixed lot of respondents representing various socio-economic and cultural backgrounds.

Realising the role of education and professional competence, the impact it creates on all the activities of individuals—this category has been further divided into "purely housewives"-120, and professionals-80. Care has been taken to find respondents representing different castes, income-groups, levels of education and levels of profession or work. Efforts have been made to find out if there is any significant difference between the political aptitude, political awareness and patterns of political activities performed by pure housewives and professionals. The data regarding personal background, perception of the self, political aptitude and political awareness have been taken together of the total respondents (200) here, but separate data from the two sub-categories regarding perception of the self, political aptitude and awareness and participation in political activities has also been collected to make a comparative analysis between the activities and behaviour of housewives as voters and professional as voters.

The first part of the Schedule contains questions designed to get information of the socio-economic and cultural (meaning education here) background of the respondents. This is a necessary exercise in all empirical studies. It is presumed that the socio-economic and cultural environment and background of the individuals is to a great extent, the deciding and designing factor of their adult activities. Political activities also are to an extent the product of these background factors of the individuals. Studies relating voting behaviour to the social variables of the respondents have been an important exercise in Political Sociology for the last four decades.

In this study also, we have tried to profile the socio-economic and cultural background of the respondents within the various categories they have been placed. Thus we start with the socio-economic and educational background of the respondents who are exclusively voters.

Socio-economic and Educational Background of the Voters Respondents

Social— Under the term 'social' the factors identified here are religion, caste and sub-caste (in the case of Hindus), Age, Place of Birth and early life spent, Marital Status and Type of the Family they live in.

Religion—As per data 187 out of the total of 200 belong to Hindu religion, ten are Muslims and three respondents are Christians. The Hindu respondents have been further divided into caste, and for the convenience of analysis are bunched together in the broader categories as follows—

1. Upper Castes	—	Brahmin, Rajput, Bhumihar and Kayastha
2. Backward Castes	—	Yadav, Kurmi, Baniya and other caste.
3. Scheduled Castes	—	Musahar, Dusadh, Chamar, Dhobi, Pasi and others.
4. Scheduled Tribes	—	Bhil, Munda, Oraon and other.

Realising the factors that the Hindu community is divided into too many castes, sub-castes, it has become a normal practice to put them in broad umbrella categories of Upper Caste, Backward and Scheduled Castes. About 96 respondents are from Upper Caste category further divided into Brahmins 25 (26.04), Rajput 24 (25%), Bhumihars 24 (25.4%) and Kayastha 23 (28.9%).

Backward Castes— Fifty four respondents belongs to Backward Castes out of which 19 are Yadav, 10 are Kurmis, 17 are Baniya and 8 belong to other Backward Castes.

Scheduled Castes— Five are Musahars while 5 are Dusadh, 2 are Chamar, and 22 belong to Dhobi, Passi, Mallah and other Scheduled Castes. The total is 34.

Scheduled Tribes— Two are 'Santhals' and one is a 'Bhil' (Table 1 and Table 2).

TABLE 1

Religion of the Respondent

Religion	*N*	%
Hindu	187	93.5
Muslim	10	5.0
Sikh	0	—
Christian	3	1.5
Total	**200**	**100.0**

TABLE 2

Caste and Sub Caste of the Respondent

Upper Caste	*N*	*BC*	*N*	*SC*	*N*	*ST*	*N*
Brahman	25 (26.04)	Yadav	19 (35.18)	Musahar	5 (14.71)	Santhal	2 (66.67)
Rajput	24 (25.00)	Kurmi	10 (18.53)	Dusadh	5 (14.71)	Bhil	1 (33.33)
Bhumihar	24 (25.20)	Baniya	17 (31.48)	Chamar	2 (5.88)		
Kayastha	24 (2390)	Other	8 (14.82)	Dhobi + Pasi other	22 (64.70)	96	
Total	96 (100.00)	Total	54 (100.00)	Total	34 (100.00)	Total	3 (100.00)

Caste has been and is increasingly more so in present a factor which is shaping the contours of politics in Bihar. For a long period, nearly forty years politics in Bihar had been dominated by Upper Caste people. It is evident also from the sample. The Backward Caste Category has been fast catching up in the road to Political Power and ever since the end of the year 1989, the Caste character of Political elites has changed dramatically and drastically. It is one factor which has to be studied and analyzed very very carefully if we want to get a true picture of politics in Bihar, even and especially in the context of women and politics in Bihar Mr. Laloo Prasad Yadav came with the slogan of "Social Justice" and was able to mobilize the backward castes under one banner. The elections of 1990, 1995 and 2000 reflect the changed caste composition of Vidhan Sabha, Council of Ministers in Bihar. Over the years there have been several caste-based splits and, currently the "Yadavs" are dominating the scene.

Age— The data reveals that 78 (39%) are from the age-group of 25-35 years and 62 (31%) are from 35-50 years age bracket. 21 (10.5) belong to 50 and above age group while 39 (19.5) are from the younger age-group 18-25 years (although this age-group is qualified to vote). The data indicates that age group of majority of the respondents come from the 25-50 years, which are the most important and active years in life, when maturity and capacity for activities are very, well blended (Table 3).

TABLE 3

Age of the Respondent

Age group	N	%
18-25	39	19.5
25-35	78	39.00
35-50	62	31.00
50-above	21	10.5
Total	**200**	**100.00**

Plan of Birth— 92 (46%) respondents were born in village, 98 (49%) in towns and 10 in city. 138 (69%) spent their early life in towns, 40 (20%) in villages and 22 in cities. At present 161 (80.5) are living in towns while 19 (9.5) are in cities at 20 (16%) are in villages. Indications are that the respondents most belong to B Class cities. As is known, there is not a single 'metropolis' in Bihar (Table 4).

TABLE 4

Place	*Place of Birth*	*Place of early life*	*Place of living present*
Village	92 (46%)	40 (200%)	20 (10%)
Town	98 (49%)	138 (69%)	161 (80.5%)
City	19 (5.%)	22 (11%)	19 (9.5%)
Total	**200(100%)**	**200(100%)**	**200(100%)**

Marital Status— As per data 189(94.5%) respondents are married out of which 159 (79.5%) were married in the age-group of 15-25 years. 10 respondents have not married and one is a widow, 37 (18.5%) respondents have married in the age-group of 25 and above. There has been no response from four respondents. The data amplifies that marriage of the girls is very much in practice in Bihar and that too around 18 years of age. Thus, political career if any has to be planned within the framework of marriage and family (Table 5 & 6).

TABLE 5

Marital Status of the Respondent

Marital Status	*N*	%
Married	189	94.5
Unmarried	10	5.0
Divorced	—	—
Widowed	1	0.5
Separated	—	—
Total	**200**	**100**

TABLE 6

Age at Marriage

Age	*N*	%
15-25	159	79.5
25 and above	37	18.5
No Answer	4	2.0
Total	**200**	**100.0**

Family Structure— 77 (38.5) respondents come from nuclear family structure while 82 (41%) the maximum come from extended families. In Bihar, extended families are very common with parents living with sons, or some relatives living for the purpose of education or job. Joint family system is still in vogue due to agricultural or business set up 41 of our respondents come from this type of family structure continuance of extended and joint family structures do create positive results for full time working women, especially women in politics (Table 7).

TABLE 7

Type of Family of the Respondent

Type of Family	*N*	%
Nuclear	77	38.5
Extended	82	41.0
Joint	41	20.5
Total	**200**	**100**

Education— 166 (83%) respondents are educated with varying levels of education. Thirty-four respondents are uneducated. 156 have received General education while 10 have been trained in Professional/ technical education. Among the 156, 19 are educated upto primary level, 44 have secondary while 53 are graduates, 16 have received Masters degree while 13 have a post-doctoral degree. Out of the 10, 5 have B.Ed, degree, one is an engineer, 2 are doctors and two have law degree (Table 8 and 9).

TABLE 8

Educational Status of the Respondent

	N	%
Educated	166	83
Uneducated	34	17
Total	**200**	**100**

TABLE 9

Level of Education

General	*N*	%	*Technical*	*N*	%
Primary	19	12.18	B.Ed.	5	50.00
Secondary	44	28.20	Engineering	1	10.00
I.A.	10	6.41	Management	—	—
Graduate	53	33.98	Medical	2	20.00
Post Graduate	16	10.25	LL.B.	2	20.00
Ph.D.	13	8.33			
Other	1	0.64			
Total	**156**	**100.00**	**Total**	**10**	**100.00**

The respondents are fairly educated, and it is excepted that they have a positive perception of the self. It will be interesting to find out how much political aptitude they have and the level of political awareness they possess.

Working Status— 80 out of the 200 respondents have full time career, about 47 (58.75%) are in service while 25 (31.25) are in business. 3 are in agriculture and 5 (6.25) do menial work (Table 10 & 11).

TABLE 10

Working Status of Respondent

	N	%
Working	80	40
Housewife	120	60
Total	**200**	**100**

TABLE 11

Occupation of the Respondent

Occupation	*N*	%
Service	47	58.75
Business	25	31.25
Agriculture	3	3.75
Menial Worker	5	6.25
Total	**80**	**100.00**

Occupation—
Service—47(58.75).

Government Service— 27 are in government service-out of these 16 are in teaching, two are medical doctors, 8 are clerks and is in fully government service.

TABLE 12

Service

Service	*Government*	*Service*	*Private*
Teaching	16(34.04)	Teaching	13(27.67)
Fully Govt.	1 (2.13)	Technical Service	2 (4.25)
Doctor	2 (4.26)	Clerk & other	2 (4.25)
Clerk	8 (17.02)	Advocate	2 (4.25)
		Journalism	1 (2.13)
Total	**27 (57.45)**	**Total**	**20(42.55)**

Private—Twenty are in private services. Thirteen are teaching in private schools, 2 are in technical jobs and one is a journalist. Two are clerks and two are advocates (Table 12).

Business— Twenty-five (31.25) are in Business. Four are in big business, two each ideal with machines and mechanicals, Twenty-one are in small business, Eleven are vegetable vendors while 10 are fruit sellers. In agriculture one is a cultivator while two are labourers.

Menial Jobs— Two each are maid servants and sweepers while one is a 'Dhobin' (Washerwoman) (Table 13).

TABLE 13

Big Business		*Small Business*		*Agriculture*		*Menial Worker*		
Machine	*Elec-trical*	*Vege-table*	*Fruit*	*Culti-vation*	*Labour*	*Dai*	*Dhobi*	*Swee-per*
2	2	11	10	1	2	2	1	2
(8.00)	(8.00)	(44.00)	(40.00)	(33.33)	(66.67)	(40.00)	(20.00)	(40.00)
	Total	**25**		**Total**	**3**	**Total**	**5**	

Total: Service-47, Business-25, Agriculture-3, Menial Worker-5 = 80

The data regarding working status indicates that the women who are in 'white collar' jobs and having a 'decent' earning are in a minority. By and large women are engaged in 'petty' jobs with low income or pay whatever the case be. Teaching especially in schools (mostly private) and clerical jobs are more frequent than income or upper level jobs like, engineering, medicine, college and university teaching and management related jobs.

Monthly Income— The maximum number 90 (45%) have a monthly income ranging between Rs. 2000-5000, while 79 have an income ranging from Rs. 5001-10000, just 17 have a monthly income above Rs. 10,000 while 14 have a Rs. 1000-2000 monthly income. The data indicates that a fairly large number of respondents belong to low and low-middle class income group 79 belong to just middle income group and only 17 have a comfortable monthly income (Table 14).

TABLE 14

Monthly Income of Respondent

Income	*N*	*%*
1000-2000	14	7.00
2000-3000	90	45.00
5000-10000	79	39.50
10000 & above	17	8.5
Total	**200**	**100.0**

Perception of the Self (as Woman)

It is often found that women have a very negative perception of the self. The social system and the socialization process cultivate the seeds of inferiority in a girl's mind from the very childhood stage—that she is a big financial burden, marriage is her only salvation and career. A daughter is inferior to the son, and not having a son is the greatest catastrophe in the family. As girls grow into woman they go on cultivating negative ideas of their 'worth', their aim in life, their ability, efficiency—their position in the family and society.

Therefore a set of questions were put to the respondents in Part II of the schedule to test how they perceive themselves, their ability, their roles in life vis-a-vis men.

TABLE 15

Self Perception of Women

Do You Believe that Women Enjoy an Equal Status with Men in Real Life?

Response	*N*	*%*
Yes	69	34.5
No	126	63.0
N.R.	5	2.5
Total	**200**	**100.0**

In response to the first Question 126 (63%) of the respondents replied that women did not enjoy equal status with men in real life. Only 69 were positive and 5 did not reply. 139 respondents

(69.5%) agreed that men were by nature made superior to women, 45 did not agree that nature made men superior while 16 did not reply (Table 15 & 16).

TABLE 16

Do You Believe that Men are by Nature Superior to Women?

Response	*N*	*%*
Yes	139	69.5
No	45	22.5
N.R.	16	8.0
Total	**200**	**100.0**

In support of their response, 50 among 139 maintained that men were physically stronger than women, while 66 (47.48%) held society responsible for giving prominence to men. 23 (16.5%) reasoned that men earned better than women. Out of 45 who did not regard that men were superior 17 (37.78) reiterated the importance of role played by women in society as being equal to that of male's 28 (62.22) reasoned that women perform the important duty of bringing up the next generation in right direction (Table 17).

TABLE 17

If Yes		*If No*	
1. They are physically stronger than women	50 (35.97%)	Women perform equally important duty in society	17 (37.78%)
2. Society gives the prominent place	66 (47.49%)	Women are important in Bringing up the next generation in right direction	28 (62.22%)
3. Usually they earn better	23 (16.55%)		
Total	**139 (100%)**	**Total**	**45 (100%)**

As education plays an important role in bringing knowledge, developing personality, preparing for a profession, it can help in the cultivation, of positive image of the 'self' in women. So, the respondents were addressed to questions related with education. 185 (92.5) respondents agreed that women should be educated, only 15 gave negative response. Regarding levels of education 90 (45.64) were in favour of graduate level education. Encouragingly 51 (27.56) showed their preference for technical education (Table 18 & 19).

TABLE 18

Should Women be Educated?

Response	*N*	%
Yes	185	92.5
No	15	7.5
Total	**200**	**100**

TABLE 19

If yes, Till Which Level?

Response	*N*	%
Primary	6	3.24
Secondary	23	12.43
Graduate	90	48.64
P.G.	15	8.10
Technical education	51	27.56
Total	**185**	**100.0**

TABLE 20

Do You Think that the Status of Educated Women in Relation to Uneducated Women is

Response	*N*	%
Superior	180	90.0
Inferior		
Equal	5	2.5
No opinion	15	7.5
Total	**200**	**100.0**

In response to the next question 180 (90%) considered the status of educated women is superior to uneducated women. Five regarded it as equal while fifteen (7.5) did not express any opinion (Table 20).

Working status with full time career gives confidence to women. Independent earning, even "modest" one hosts their confidence. So the respondents were asked to answer certain questions in this direction. 135(67.5) respondents were in favour of full time career for women (67.5) while 49 (24.5) were against it, 16 respondents did not reply. Among the 145, 58 reasoned that it gives confidence, 49 saw it as giving economic independence while 28 reasoned that the social status of such women is enhanced. Among those who disagreed, 19 (38.78) reasoned that it would break the family while 27 (55.10) thought that by temperament and physical ability, women would find a full time job tough (Table 21 &22).

TABLE 21

Do You Believe in Full Time Career for Women?

Response	N	%
Yes	135	67.5
No	49	24.5
N.R.	16	8.0
Total	**200**	**100.0**

TABLE 22

	If yes, why?		*If no, why?*	
1.	It gives confidence	58 (38.41)	Economic independence break the family	19 (38.78)
2.	It gives economic independence	49 (32.46)	Temperament and physical ability may make the job tough	27 (55.10)
3.	It gives better status in Society	44 (29.14)	Any other	3 (6.12)
	Total	**151 (100.00)**	**Total**	**49 (100.00)**

If we compare the responses of housewives and professionals we find some differences, while among professionals 52 out of 80 believed in the equality of status between men and women, among housewives only 17 out of 120 gave this response. 98 saw the comparative status as unequal, meaning thereby that women saw their status as inferior to men As regards superiority of men given by nature 51.2% among professionals and 81.6% among housewives believed that the male was made superior by nature to woman. Again there is a wide gap in the response. As regards education, its importance for women and a full time career for women, the responses flow almost in the same direction. Majority believe that the status of educated women in relation to uneducated women is superior.

Political Aptitude

Aptitude to a certain extent directs individuals towards particular activities. No doubt aptitude can be cultivated and nurtured through various methods but if it is present naturally, the activity performed can have excellent quality. But individuals live in a society among people, and they do have to perform certain functions in order to exist in a good way. Political activities are such activities which citizens have to perform rightly because most of us are living in Representative democratic politics, and citizens have the power and the corresponding duty to choose their representatives for governance, take part themselves in governance and so on and so forth. Thus, it is necessary to have an 'aptitude' towards things "political" women have been since centuries marginalized and ignored in political arena because of the actuated myth that women hand no aptitude for "political things".

So, a set of questions were addressed to the respondents to get an idea about their "political aptitude".

Out of the total respondents 28 (14%) strongly approved of a political career for women while 35 (17.5) agreed. Taken together 63 respondents agree to women having political career. 87 (43.5) disapproved while 26 strongly disapproved. Taken together 113 respondents did not agree to political career for women. Another 24 did not even respond to this important question (Table 23).

TABLE 23

Would You Approve of Political Career for Women?

	N	%
Strongly approve	28	14.00
Approve	35	17.5
Strongly disapprove	26	13.0
Disapprove	87	43.5
No Response	24	12.0
Total	**200**	**100.0**

Among those who approved 36 (57.14) supported it because entering politics would help the improvement of life-conditions, and 27 (42.86) thought that if women entered politics it would be cleaned. Among those who disapprove 56 (50.45) thought that it will create tension in the family, 11 (9.9) believed that the women's image will be damaged. Seventeen (15.31) reasoned that women by temperament and physical ability will find the work tough. About 27 (24.32) did not approve because of growing use of money and muscle power in Politics (Table 24).

TABLE 24

If approve, why?	*N*	*If disapprove why?*	*N*
1. Entering politics will improve their life condition	36 (57.14)	1. It creates tension in family	56 (50.45)
2. Women's entrance may cleanse politics	27 (42.86)	2. Damages their image	11 (9.91)
		3. Lack of tempera-ment and physical ability for tough job	17 (15.32)
		4. It involves a lot of money increasing use of muscle power in politics	27 (24.32)
		5. Any other	2 (1.77)
Total	**63 (100.00)**	**Total**	**113 (100.00)**

The respondents were asked if women will be successful in leadership positions? Again, the response of 106 was negative and the reasons given by 41 (38.68) were that women lack social inter action, by 34 that women cannot work that hard and are not tough enough. 17 thought that entry into Politics will be damaging to image and character while 14 were against it because of growing criminalisation of Politics.

94 (47%) were positive and among the 47 reasoned that women are on equal footing with men in this regard. 41 reasoned that our constitution gives equal political rights to men and women, and 5 believed that her achievements in political field will prove her success (Table 25 & 26).

TABLE 25

Would Women be Successful in Political Leadership Position?

Response	*N*	*%*
Yes	94	47
No	106	53
Total	**200**	**100**

TABLE 26

If yes, why	*N (%)*	*If no, why*	*N (%)*
She is an equal footing with men in the regard	48 (51.07)	Lack of social interaction	41 (38.68)
Our constitution guarantees equal political rights to men and women	41 (43.62)	Lack of land work and Toughness	34 (32.07)
Her achievements in pol. field itself	5 (5.31)	Damaging to image and character	17 (16.04)
		Criminalization of politics	14 (13.20)
Total	**94 (100.00)**	**Total**	**106 (100.00)**

A glance at the responses indicates that the respondents do not have very strong aptitude for Politics. The social considerations like family tensions damage to image and character, dominate women's choice of a political career. They display lack of confidence in their ability to do jobs related to politics. Increased criminalisation of politics and increasing use of money in politics deter women from politics. As we have seen nearly 106 do not believe that women could be successful as political leaders. If we compare the responses of professionals and housewives, 41 among 80 professionals were against political career for women. Among housewives 72 disapproved among 120.

Political Awareness

The respondents were tested for their political awareness. They were served with list of mixed names and asked to identify politically important women and men in Indian Politics and politics of Bihar. They were also asked to identify the form of present Indian government, parties of national and regional level, party ruling Bihar, opposition party etc.

Among the five names listed 195 (97.5) identified Indira Gandhi as a Political leader, 34 (17%) could identify Begum Khalida Zia. Strongly enough, the famous environmental activist Medha Patekar was identified by as many as 61 (30.5) respondents (Table 27).

TABLE 27

Listed Below are the Names of Five Important Women Who Among Them are Politically Important?

Name of women	*N*	%
Mother Teressa	5	2.5
Begum Khalida Zia	34	17.0
Indira Gandhi	195	97.5
Margeret Thatcher	61	30.5
Medha Patekar	61	30.5

109 (54.5%) respondents did not agree that the rule of Indira Gandhi as Prime Minister did raise the over all status of women in India. 91 responded in the positive.

Out of the 91, 20 believed that Indira Gandhi became role-model for women, 33 (36.26) maintained that she defied the 'myth' that women are no good in Politics. 58 (63.74) felt that it did help to change the social attitude towards women (Table 28 & 29).

TABLE 28

Did Indira Gandhi as Prime Minister Raise the Overall Status of Indian Women?

Response	*N*	%
Yes	91	45.5
No	109	54.5
Total	**200**	**100.0**

TABLE 29

If yes, why?	*N*	%
She became a role model	20	21.98
Defied the myth that women are no good in politics	33	36.26
Social Attitude toward women changed	38	41.76
Total	**91**	**100.0**

Form of Indian Government

175 (87.5) respondents correctly identified it Parliamentary, only 4 said it was Presidential, Thirteen (6.5) described it as Federal (Table 30).

TABLE 30

What Pattern of Government Does India Have at Present?

Pattern	*N*	%
Parliamentary	175	87.5
Presidential	4	2.0
Unitary	—	—
Federal	13	6.5
N.R.	8	4.0
Total	**200**	**100.0**

192 (96%) respondents regarded Democracy as the form of government most suitable for India. Regarding five important national parties, 189 (94.5) named Congress I, 188 B.J.P., 184 Janata Dal, 158 C.P.M. and 141 (70.3) C.P.I. (Table 31 & 32).

TABLE 31

What Form of Government Do You Consider to be More Suitable for India?

Response	*N*	%
Democracy	192	96.0
Aristocracy	2	1.0
Dictatorship	—	—
N.R.	6	3.0
Total	**200**	**100.0**

TABLE 32

Name Five Important Parties of National Level

National Party	*N*	%
B.J.P.	188	94.0
Congress	189	94.5
C.P.M.	158	79.0
C.P.I.	141	70.5
J.D.	184	92.0

As for Regional Parties, 189 (94.5) named Rashtriya Janata Dal (R.J.D.), 126 (63%) identified Shiv Sena and 80 (40%) identified Jharkhand Mukti Morcha (Table 33). The respondents were given a mixed list of names of important women in various fields to cross-check their awareness—Again Congress I was identified by 185 (92.5), 184 (92%) identified B.J.P. while 160 identified, Janata Dal. The C.P.M. was identified by 126 (635) and CPI ML by 147 (73.5%) (Table 33 & 34).

TABLE 33

Name Five Important Regional Parties, Including Bihar

R.J.D.	189	94.5
Shiv Sena	126	63.0
AIDMK	53	26.3
B.S.P.	63	31.5
Akali Dal	64	32.0
Samta	62	31.0
Telegu Desham	75	37.5
J.M.M.	80	40.0

TABLE 34

Given Below are the Names of Political Parties—Which among them are National Parties?

Name of the party	*N*	*%*
R.J.D.	6	3.0
J.M.M.	38	19.0
B.S.P.	22	11.0
B.J.P.	184	92.0
Samta Party	94	47.0
CPI ML	147	73.5
J.D.	160	80.0
D.M.K.	13	6.5
Congress	185	92.5
C.P.M.	126	63.0
Forward Block	10	5.0
Jan Mukti Morcha	2	1.0

A list of ten famous person of the World was given to the respondents and they were asked to identify political leaders among them 198 (99%) named Mahatma Gandhi, and 195 (97.5) were for Jawahar Lal Nehru, 163 (81.5) knew Jai Prakash Narain, while 147 (73.5) could identify Lal Bahadur Shastri (Table 35).

TABLE 35

Given Below are the Names Often Important Person of the World Who among them Were Political Leaders?

Name of Person	*N*	%
Martin Luther King	6	3.0
Mother Teressa	7	3.5
Mahatma Gandhi	198	99.0
Karl Marx	75	37.5
Swami Vivekanand	—	—
Jai Prakash Narain	163	81.5
Mao-tse-Tung	68	34.00
Ravindra Nath Tagore	2	10
Lal Bahadur Shastri	147	73.5
Pt. Ravi Shankar	—	—
Jawahar Lal Nehru	195	97.5

The responses show that the respondents have a fair awareness of political leaders.

While naming five important women political leaders in India, Indira Gandhi was mentioned by 190 (95%) other names mentioned were: Vijayalaxmi Pandit by 93, Sonia Gandhi by 78, Sushma Swaraj by 68, Margaret Alva by 65, Tarkeshwari Sinha by 66 respondents (Table 36).

TABLE 36

Name Five Important Women in Indian Politics

Name	*N*	%
Indira Gandhi	190	95.0
Sarojini Naidu	51	25.5
Vijaya Laxmi Pandit	93	46.3
Sonia Gandhi	78	39.0
Margaret Alva	65	32.5
Sushma Swaraj	68	34.0
Rabri Devi	44	22.0
Tarkeshwari Sinha	66	33.0

To cross-check their awareness, the respondents were asked to pinpoint women political leaders from a list of women important in various fields and again Indira Gandhi was identified by 190 (95%) while Sarojini Naidu was identified by 107 (53.5%) (Table 37).

TABLE 37

Given Below are the Names of Some Important Women in India, Who among them Were Political Leaders?

Name	N	%
Medha Pateker	53	26.3
M.S. Shubhalaxmi	—	—
Indira Gandhi	190	95.0
Sarojini Naidu	107	59.5

Coming to Bihar the respondents were asked to name five important women political leaders in Bihar. Rabri Devi topped the list named by 193 (96.5%) respondents, Uma Pandey came next with 143 (61.5%) respondents, Kanti Singh was named by 102 (51 %) while Rita Verma was named by 95 (47.5%) (Table 38).

TABLE 38

Name Five Important Women in Politics in Bihar

Name	N	%
Rabri Devi	193	96.5
Rita Verma	95	47.5
Kanti Singh	102	51.0
Tarkeshwari Sinha	53	51.3
Uma Pandey	143	71.5
Kishori Sinha	53	21.5
Krishna Shahi	62	31.0

When asked to list five male political leaders of Bihar, 196 respondents named Laloo Prasad Yadav, Ram Vilas Pawan was named by 171 (85.5%) respondents and Jagannath Mishra by 153 (76.5), Dr. Rajendra Prasad was named only by 71 (35.5) while

Karpoori Thakur was named by 87 (43.5%) respondents (Table 39).

TABLE 39

Name Five Important Political Leaders in Bihar

Name	N	%
Laloo Prasad Yadav	191	95.5
Ram Vilash Paswan	171	85.5
Karpoori Thakur	87	43.5
Shibu Soren	58	29.0
Jagannath Mishra	153	76.5
Dr. Rajendra Prasad	71	35.5
K.B. Sahay	56	28.0

The respondents correctly identified the ruling party in 1998-99, 186 (93%) identified Rashtriya Janata Dal as the ruling and 180 (90%) identified Bharatiya Janata Party as the main opposition party in Bihar (98-99), 180 (90%) respondent were assured that the Government would complete its 5 year term, which it did and the next elections were held in the year 2000 (Table 40, 41 & 42).

TABLE 40

Which Party is Ruling in Bihar at Present (1998-99)

Name of the party	N	%
R.J.D.	186	93.0
N.R.	14	7.0
Total	**200**	**100.0**

TABLE 41

Which Party is in the Opposition in Bihar Vidhan Sabha at Present (1998-99)

Name of the party	N	%
B.J.P.	180	90.0
N.R.	20	10.0
Total	**200**	**100.0**

TABLE 42

Do You Think that the Present Government Will Complete its Five Year Term?

Response	*N*	%
Yes	180	90.0
No	—	—
NR	20	10.0
Total	**200**	**100.0**

Opinion was quite divided and negative as regards a separate Jharkhand State. 97 (48.5%) were against and as many as 52 (26%) were silent on this issue. It is clear from the response that this idea was not favourable to the respondents then. Nevertheless, a separate Jharkhand State did come into existence on 15.11.2000 (Table 43).

TABLE 43

Are You in Favour of a Separate Jharkhand State

Response	N	%
Yes	51	25.5
No	97	48.5
N.R.	52	26.0
Total	**200**	**100.0**

Caste is a dominant player of the political scenes in Bihar for decades, and has reached its pinnacle in the last one decade. 51 respondents (25.5%) agreed that cast is the bane of politics in Bihar, but surprisingly 94 (47%) do not agree and as many as 55 have not replied.

The reasons given by those who agreed were (1) that caste-based voting prevents the entry of able persons in government-49 respondents, (2) beads to social tensions-by 20 (3) the Government does not work for the welfare of all-by 29.

Those who favoured caste based politics gave their own reasons-23 favour it because it will demolish the hegemony of upper castes in Bihar politics. 15 believe that the backward and lower caste people will get their chance in politics, while according to 99, it will bring social justice (Table 44 & 45).

TABLE 44

Caste is the Bane of Politics in Bihar - Do You Agree?

Response	*N*	*%*
Yes	51	25.5
No	94	47.0
N.R.	55	27.5
Total	**200**	**100.0**

TABLE 45

If yes	*N*	*%*	*If No*	*N*	*%*
1. Voting on caste basis prohibitable person to come in politics	49	50.00	1. It will demolish upper caste hegemony of Bihar politics	13	27.67
2. It leads to social tension	20	20.40	2. The backward and lower caste will get a change to enter politics	15	31.91
3. The Govt. does not work for welfare of people	29	29.60	3. It will bring socket justice	19	40.42
Total	**98**	**100.00**	**Total**	**47**	**100.00**

The respondents were asked to evaluate politics in Bihar and respond if it was totally corrupt 100 (50) agreed that it was totally corrupt. 60 (30%) do not regard politics in Bihar as corrupt. 40 did not respond. Those who agreed gave the following reason-50 agreed that voting is done on caste consideration, 30 believed that votes are freely 'sold', and 20 maintained that there is increasing use of muscle power in politics. Those who did not consider politics in Bihar to be corrupt head their own set of reasons-20 agreed that elections are dominated by money power everywhere, 10 reasoned that caste is a dominant factor not only in Bihar politics but all over India.

30 strongly believed that the backward and scheduled caste people were getting a fair access in Politics (Table 46 and 47).

TABLE 46

Do You Agree that Politics in Bihar is Totally Corrupt?

Response	*N*	*%*
Yes	100	50.0
No	60	30.0
N.R.	40	20.0
Total	**200**	**100.0**

TABLE 47

If yes	*N*	*%*	*If No*	*N*	*%*
1. Voting is done on caste considerations	50	50.0	1. Election are dominated by money power every where.	20	33.33
2. Votes are sold for money	30	30.0	2. Caste is a dominant factor not only in Bihar but in whole India	10	16.67
3. Muscle power is used in politics	20	20.0	3. Backward and SC are getting a fair chance in politics at present	30	50.0
Total	**100**	**100.0**	**Total**	**60**	**100.0**

Lastly the respondents were asked to ascertain the marks of a good government. 125 respondents listed "Stability" as the mark of a good government, while 70 (35%) regarded that it should be free of corruption and 63 (31.5%) thought that such a government should have concern for the Welfare of all citizens (Table 48)

TABLE 48

What is the Mark of a Good Government?

Mark of Good Govt.	*N*	*%*
Stability	125	62.5
Free of corruption	70	35.00
Concern for the Welfare of all citizen	63	31.5
Any other	6	3.0

The responses indicate that the respondents have clear idea about important political leaders both at the national and State level of Bihar. Most of them know about the forms of government, and the form of present National Government. They also have a good idea about National and Regional Parties. Caste has been acknowledged as a dominant factor in politics in Bihar. It is disappointing that a reasonable number have tried to justify it in the name of 'Social Justice". Most disheartening is the response about corruption in Bihar politics, the manner in which about half (60 No. and 40 N.R.) have justified this corruption.

Participation in Politics

Part IV B contained questions regarding political participation. The respondents in this category are essentially voters, therefore they were served with questions related to voting in elections

The first question however was asked to asses their awareness about the importance of voting. They were asked to tell whether voting was necessary in a Democracy and why. All the respondents agreed that voting was very important in Democracy 128 (64%) respondents answered in the positive because Democracy is the government of the people, for the people and by the people. 40 respondents (20%) agreed that voting indicates people's choice of their representatives. 28 (14%) reasoned that it is necessary for the functioning of Indirect Democracy (Table 49).

TABLE 49

Voting is Important for Democracy—Why?

	N	%
Democracy is the Govt. of the people for the people by the people	128	64.0
Voting indicates people's choice of their representatives	40	20.0
Voting is necessary in Indirect Democracy	28	14.0
Any other	4	2.0
Total	**200**	**100.0**

The respondents were asked next if they had ever voted in any General Election and the response was that 130 (65%) out of the total 200 had voted, 91 out of 130 (70%) had first voted in Lok Sabha Elections while 39 (30%) had first voted in Vidhan Sabha Elections (Table 50). Out of the 91 who voted first in Lok Sabha Election the maximum number (14) voted in 1977 and then again the same number first voted in 1996 (Table 51).

TABLE 50

Have You Voted in Any Election?

Response	*N*	*%*	*Lok Sabha*	*Vidhan Sabha*
Yes	130	65.0	91 (70.0)	39 (30.0)
No	70	35.0		
Total	**200**	**100.0**	**91**	**39(30.0)**

TABLE 51

Name First Election, Year, and Party of Your Voting Lok Sabha

Year	*N (%)*	*Party*
1952		
1957	1 (1.09)	Congress
1962	1 (1.09)	Congress
1967	3 (3.29)	Congress
1971	6 (6.5)	V.K.P.-1, Congress-2, JP-2, Jan Sangh-1
1977	14 (15.38)	JP-12, Congress-1, IFP-1
1980	2 (2.19)	JP-1, Congress-1
1984	13 (14.26)	Congress-10, BHP-2, CPI-1
1989	13 (14.28)	IPF-3, JD-5, BJP-3, JP-1, Congress-I
1991	11 (12.08)	JD-3, BHP-4, Congress-2, JMM-1, IPF-1
1996	14 (15.36)	JD-5, BJP-7, Samta-2
1998	13 (14.28)	BJP-9, IPF-1, Samta Party-1, Janata Dal-2
Total	**91 (100.0)**	

The reason for more voting in 1977 may be attributed to the tremendous political changes taking place at that time. The hegemony of Congress Party was being challenged and an alternative force in the form of Janata Party had emerged. People wanted some change in the political scenario and women of Bihar who had just emerged from their participation and experiences in Total revolution did not lag behind in performing their duty as voters. As can be seen in the table, 14 out of 12 had votes for Janata Party

As regards first voting in Vidhan Sabha Elections, as many as 36 voted in '95 Vidhan Sabha Election. The table below indicates a clean polarization of voting in favour of Bharatiya Janata Party and Janata Dal (Table 52).

TABLE 52

Name the Election, and Party of First Voting Vidhan Sabha

Year	*N (%)*	*Party*
1969	2 (5.12)	Janata Party, P.S.P.
1985	1 (2.57)	C.P.I.
1995	36 (92.00)	BJP-17, JD-17, Congress-2
Total	**30 (100.00)**	

Lok Sabha Election 1988

The respondents were asked about their participation in '98 Lok Sabha Elections.* Out of 200, 123 (61.5) respondents had voted while 77 (38.5) had not voted. Among the 123 who voted, the maximum number 64 (52.03) voted for B.J.P. while 25 (20.32) voted for Rashtriya Janata Dal (R.J.D.). As regards reasons for voting, 30 (24.39) voted due to the charismatic personality of the candidate, 30 (24.39) voted on party image and 30 (24.39) voted because of a particular party's programme and election manifesto. As many as 20 (16.26) admitted to having voted on caste considerations. Two had voted on the basis of religion while 11 (8.94) voted on the suggestions of others, may be a relative, colleague or a friend (Table 53 and 54).

**NOTE:* The data was collected between '98 and early '99 therefore questions were asked about '98 Elections the last, till that time.

TABLE 53

Were You a Voter in 1998 Lok Sabha Election? Did You Vote?

Response	*N*	*%*
Yes	123	61.5
No	77	38.5
Total	**200**	**100.0**

TABLE 54

Name of the party	*N*	*Reason for voting*	*N*
B.J.P.	64 (52.03)	Charismatic personally	30 (24.39)
Samata Party	10 (8.13)	Party Image	30 (24.39)
R.J.D.	25 (20.37)	Party programme and manifesto	30 (24.39)
Congress	6 (4.88)	Caste	20 (16.26)
C.P.I.	2 (1.63)	Religion	2 (1.62)
CPM ML	10 (8.13)	Suggested by others	11 (8.94)
J.D.	5 (4.06)		
J.M.M.	1 (0.81)		
Total	**123** **(100.0)**	**Total**	**123** **(100.0)**

Assembly Elections '95 (Bihar)

The respondents were asked about their voting participation in, 95. 103 (51.5) respondents had taken part in election as voters, while 97 had not voted. Amount the voters 43 had voted for B.J.P. while 36 for Janata Dal. Congress I was voted for by nine. The reasons provided were personality of the contestant by 36, party image by 43 (41.74), 5 voted on party manifesto and programme, nineteen voted on Caste considerations (Table 55 and 56).

TABLE 55

Were You Voter in 1995 Bihar Vidhan Sabha Election

Response	*N*	*%*
Yes	103	51.5
No	97	48.51
Total	**200**	**100.0**

TABLE 56

If yes, Name the Party, and Reasons for Voting

Name of the party	*N*	*Reason for voting*	*N*
B.J.P.	43 (41.74)	Charismatic personality	36 (34.95)
J.D.	36 (34.95)	Party image	43 (41.74)
Congress	9 (8.74)	Party programme and manifesto	5 (4.85)
Samata Party	5 (4.85)	Caste	19 (18.43)
J.M.M.	2 (1.94)	Religion	
C.P.I.	2 (1.94)	Suggested by others	
C.P.M.	1 (0.97)		
Total	**103** **(100.0)**		**103** **(100.0)**

The responses reveal that women in our sample have voted in reasonably satisfactory numbers. Considering the fact that Bihar has been for long one among the five lowest mobilizer States of women voters, 50% voting by women can be regarded as satisfactory. The voting pattern shows that at least in Bihar Vidhan Sabha Elections '95, women's votes are quite clearly split between the B.J.P. and Janata Dal. The Third Party which has been able to mobilize women's vote to some extent is CPI ML, and Samata Party. The picture is almost similar in '98 Lok Sabha elections, J.D. vote have been split between R.J.D. and J.D.

Canvassing

The response has been very poor. Out of the total of 200 respondents only 20 have ever canvassed for any party. It amounts to just 10% of the total respondents. Among the twenty, 16 belong to the professional category. Among the 120 housewives only four have participated in canvassing. So, in general, it is not a common practice for women to take part in canvassing. Women have not been mobilized as "Canvassers". May be, it is due to the fact that the society does not appreciate women going door to door for canvassing. Excepting a few Congress women leaders in the earlier phase and the women from left parties, especially CPI ML in recent elections, and to some extent B.J.P. have taken part in this exercise (Table 57).

TABLE 57

Did You Take Part in Canvassing for Any Party in the Election?

Year	*N*	*Party*	*Reasons*
1957	2 (10.00)	Congress	Party programme
1969	2 (10.00)	Congress	Party programme
1991	3 (15.00)	CPM, JD, IPF	Party programme personality of the candidate.
1996	5 (25.00)	JD, IPF, CPI ML, CPM	For fun
1998	8 (40.00)	BJP, RJD, CPI ML	Personality of the candidate, party programme.
Total	**20 (10.00)**		

To evaluate their observation power of the present set up during elections the respondents were asked whether they saw certain elements in operation during elections. Hundred (50%) respondents had observed castes in and communalism on display. 120 reported "Goondaism" prevalent during elections. 120 respondents also witnessed too much use of money and "muscle power" during elections. The picture depicted of the Election scene as 'grim.' Too much violence, squandering money, Goonda elements operating freely. It is due to this sort of environment that women 'shun' away from exercising their voting rights (Table 58).

TABLE 58

Did You Notice that the Following Elements Operating During Elections

Response	N	%
Casteism and communalism	100	50.00
Goondaism	120	60.00
Groupism	50	25.00
Extravagent use of money	120	60.00
Use of muscle power	120	60.00

Voting behaviour of women in Bihar, as elsewhere in India is determined to a considerable extent by the hold of the 'Patriarchy'—patriarch or the male head of the family. Families which are politically oriented, encourage their women to take part in voting. But a considerable percentage of families especially of middle class do not like their women to go to the 'booths' for casting their votes. Women from lower income-group-workers, in small jobs, have been mobilized by the Political Parties to a certain extent to vote in elections. The upper middle class and upper class women, even professionals are reluctant to go and cast their votes. The environment of acute violence and 'goodaism' during voting is a major deterrent. The law and order situation is deplorable and the police play like puppets to the tune of political leaders. If the law and order situation is under control, the number of women voters is certainly expected to go up.

All the questions in Part IV C of the schedule were not addressed to the voters. Just a few questions were placed before them for response which are as follows:

1. Do you desire to contest elections? If yes, why?
2. Do you agree with 33 % reservation for women in Lok Sabha and Vidhan Sabha? If yes, why? If No, why?
3. Do you approve of Anti-Defection Law? If yes, why? If 'no', why?

Desire to Contest Elections

Out of the total of 200 respondents only 52 (40) did desire to contest elections some tune while 135 (67.5) did not wish to contest elections. There was not much difference between the response of housewives and professionals. Only 14 (17.5) out of 80 gave a positive response while 53 (66.25) said 'no' and 13 (16.25) did not respond at all. Among the 120 'housewives' just 38 (31.6) said 'yes' while 82 (68.3) gave a negative reply.

Regarding reasons already listed, among those who did desire to contest elections 39 (28) housewives and 11 professional wanted to serve people. Three wanted to contest elections for power; nine for social prestige.

Among these who said 'No', 20 agreed that there was lack of funds, 44 reasoned that Political Parties are apathetic towards giving 'Party tickets' to women. 40, respondents did not want to enter elections because of increasing violence during elections. Thirty one had no liking for this sort of activity (Table 59 and 60).

TABLE 59

Do You Desire to Contest Election?

Response	*N*	*%*
Yes	52	26.0
No	135	67.5
N.R.	13	6.5
Total	**200**	**100.0**

TABLE 60

If Yes, Why? If No, Why?

If yes, why	*N*	*%*	*If no, why*	*N*	*%*
Desire to serve people	39	75.0	Of lack of funds	20	14.81
For power	3	5.76	Apathy of Political parties in given ticket	44	32.59
For social prestige	9	17.30	Increasing violence during election	40	29.62
Any other	1	1.92			
Total	**52**	**100.0**	**Total**	**135**	**100.0**

It can be concluded that women are not very keen to contest elections due to the reasons which do have content. Lack of funds among women, increasing violence and the attitude of the parties towards women are factors which are very visible. Even women with capability do not want to enter election politics.

33 Per Cent Reservation for Women

There is overwhelming support by respondents on this issue. Out of 200, 120 respondents favour 33 % reservation for women, among the professionals 47 (58%) are in favour of reservation while among the housewives 73 (60.8) are in support for reservation. So, although 135 respondents do not want to contest elections, they should not be regarded as "apathetic" to politics. If they do not want to contest elections, it is mainly because 'Politics' has acquired a very negative Character. Especially, election process has become very corrupt and violent. Women find the whole atmosphere very hostile. They would join 'Politics' in large numbers if 'avenues' are opened for them through reservation.

About 57 (47.5) reason that it will make the entry into "Politics" easier. Eighteen agree with the reason that parties will be forced to put up more women candidates in Elections. Six felt that the presence of women in Lok Sabha and Vidhan Sabha will be felt. Thirty five respondents agreed with the reason that the problems of women will be highlighted in Lok Sabha and Vidhan Sabha and remedies will be explored.

TABLE 61

What is Your Reaction Towards 33% Reservation for Women in Lok Sabha and Vidhan Sabha?

Response	*N*	%
Yes	120	60.00
No	72	36.00
N.R.	8	4.00
Total	**200**	**100.00**

Among those who were against it 12 supported the reason that reservation is against the principle of Democracy, 38 agreed that only elite women will benefit from reservation. Ten maintained that problems of common women will not be attended to. Seven thought that it will affect the smooth working of Lok Sabha. Three thought that inexperienced women will get into these bodies (Table 61 and 62).

TABLE 62

If yes	N	%	*If no*	N	%
It will make easy for women to fight election	57	47.5	It is against the principle of Democracy	N	%
Parties will be forced to put up women candidate	18	15.0	Only elite worker will be benefited	38	52.78
Their presence in the Lok Sabha and Vidhan Sabha will felt	6	5.00	Problem of the common women will not be litigated	10	13.89
They will bring up problem of women in these Sabha and force to remove it	35	29.16	It will affect smooth working to the Sabha	7	9.72
Struggle for Right	4	3.33	Because most of the women will be unexperienced	3	4.17
Total	120	100.0	Total	72	100.00

Anti Defection Law

Seventy respondents approved of Anti-defection law, 60 (30%) disapproved while as many as 70 (35%) did not reply. Especially, there was hardly any response from the housewives. Among those who agreed with the reasons for their approval of this law. 20 (28.57) expected that it will make the Government more stable while 20 (28.57) were hopeful that corruption among legislators will be controlled. Thirty respondents were hopeful that it will increase dedication to and discipline in the Party. Among those who disapproved as many 25 hoped that Party Leaders will not act arbitrarily. Twenty-five reasoned that small parties (groups) will get a chance to reach the top. Ten expected that secondary level leaders will get chance to move upward (Table 63 & 64).

TABLE 63

Do You Approve of Anti Defection Law?

Response	*N*	%
Yes	70	35.0
No	60	30.0
N.R.	70	35.0
Total	**200**	**100.0**

TABLE 64

If Yes		*If no*	
Government will be more stable	20 (28.57)	Party leader will not be act arbitrarily	25 (41.66)
It will control corruption	20 (28.57)	Small parties will get a chance to reach the top	25 (41.66)
It will increase dedication on the party	30 (42.86)	Secondary leader will get a chance to reach the top	10 (16.67)
Total	**70 (100.0)**	**Total**	**60 (100.0)**

A perusal of the responses by this category of respondents reveals that women have not been able to perform their duty as voters because, to a certain extent they do lack the aptitude and awareness required for the exercise of this important political right. However, the situational factors have to be taken into account, and more importantly, an improvement in the law and order situation and a effective 'curb' on increasing violence during elections needs to be made urgently. Women fear violence and 'goondaism' on "Polling booths" more than their apathy towards voting. If the election scenario changes and becomes more and more orderly and free from violence, the number of women voters will certainly "go up".

5

Women Political Activists

This chapter contains the responses of political activists—women who are active members of any political party, are holding some post in the party hierarchy or are working without any post for the Party as propagators of party ideology, and mobilisers of people, especially women at the grass root level. Such women normally are aware of their party programmes, take part in Morchas, Dharna, Processions and meetings. Many work in the "Mahila Wing" or "Women's Wing" of their party, organizing women for meetings and procession in order to register women's reaction on current issues of general nature and also women specific issues such as crimes against women, the failure of the Administration in Controlling violence against women, price rise of essential commodities, the issue of reservation for women in Legislative bodies. Women associated with Left Parties especially CPI ML are very active in mobilizing women for expression of their resentment against government policies, spread of education and political awareness among women both rural and urban at the grass root level. This category includes well educated and professionals as well as poor uneducated, illiterate or semi-literate women doing small jobs from farm labour to vegetables vendors. The schedule has been divided into the four following sections in the following manner:

(a) Socio-economic and cultural (educational) background of the respondents.

(b) Perception of the self (as women).

(c) Political aptitude and political awareness, and

(d) Political activities, career history, opinions on current political issues and controversies.

Socio-economic and Cultural (Educational) Background of Respondents

As socio-economic and cultural environment shapes individual behaviour, we start with the socio-economic and cultural background of respondents.

Social

Religion. Among the total 50 respondents, 45 (90%) are Hindus and 5 (10%) are Christians. The Hindu respondents have been further categorized of upper castes, Backward Castes and Scheduled Castes, and one separate category of Scheduled Tribes. 26 belong to upper caste (52%), 17 to Backward Caste (37%), 4 to Scheduled Caste (8%) and 3 to the 4th category of Scheduled Tribes (Table 1 and 2).

TABLE 1

Religion of the Respondent

Religion	*Frequency*	*Percentage*
Hindu	45	90%
Muslim	—	—
Sikh	—	—
Christian	5	10%
Total	**50**	**100.00**

TABLE 2

Caste of the Respondent

Caste	*Frequency*	*Percentage*
Upper Caste	26	52
Backward Caste	17	34
Scheduled Caste	4	8
Scheduled Tribe	3	6
Total	**50**	**100.00**

Upper Castes

Brahmins, Bhumihars, Rajputs and Kayasthas are bunched together in Upper Castes. Among 26, 10 are Brahmins, 7 are Rajputs, 4 are from Bhumihar Caste and 5 (five) respondents are Kayastha. Very clearly, 38.4% of the Upper Caste respondents are Brahmins. One could say that 52% of the respondents belong to Upper Castes.

Backward Castes

Out 17, 4 are Yadav, 4 belong to Kurmi Caste, 4 are Baniyas and 5 belong to the other backward castes—a total of 17 (34%) belong to Backward Castes.

Scheduled Castes

One each are from Dusadh and Chamar Caste while 2 come from Pasi, Dhobi and other castes.

Scheduled Tribes

Three respondents belonging one each to Bhil, Munda, Oraon Tribes are in this category (Table 3).

TABLE 3

Upper Caste	*N (%)*	*B.C.*	*N (%)*	*S.C.*	*N (%)*	*S.T.*	*N (%)*
Brahmin	10 (38.46)	Yadav	4 (23.52)	Musahar	—	Santhal	—
Rajput	7 (26.92)	Kurmi	4 (23.52)	Dusadh	1 (25.00)	Uraon	1 (33.33)
Bhumihar	4 (15.38)	Baniya	4 (23.52)	Chamar	1 (25.00)	Bhil	1 (33.33)
Kayastha	5 (19.23)	Other	5 (29.41)	Pasi, Dhobi Other	2 (50.00)	Other Munda	1 (33.33)
Total	**2 (100.00)**	**Total**	**17 (100.00)**	**Total**	**4 (100.00)**	**Total**	**3 (100.00)**

Age

26 (52%) respondents; belong to the age-group of 25-35 years. Fifteen belong to 35-50 age group, 4 are from 18-25 years age group while 5 are above 50. Most of the respondents are in the most active, creative and constructive age-group (Table 4).

TABLE 4

Age of the Respondent

Age Group	*Frequency*	*Percentage*
18-25	4	8
25-35	26	12
35-50	15	30
50 & above	6	10
Total	**50**	**100.00**

Place of Birth

32 respondents were born in towns while 11 were born in villages and 7 in cities. 37 spent their early life in towns while nine were in cities and only 4 spent their early life in villages. None were living in village at present. 32 are at present living in towns while only 8 (16%) are living in cities The respondents mostly belong to sub-urban background (Table 5).

TABLE 5

Place of Birth, Live of Respondent

Place	*Place of birth*	*Live most of Easy life*	*Live at present*
Village	11 (22%)	4 (8%)	—
Town	32 (64%)	37 (74%)	32 (64%)
City	7 (14%)	9(18%)	8 (16%)
Total	**50 (100.00)**	**50 (100.00)**	**50 (100.00)**

Marriage

45 out of the 50 respondents are married, only 5 are unmarried. All the 45 respondents got married in the age-group of 15-25. One could say that they got married reasonably early, and are pursuing political activities within the frame-work of marriage (Table 6 and 7).

TABLE 6

Marital Status of Respondent

Status	*Frequency*	*Percentage*
Married	45	90
Unmarried	5	10
Divorced	—	—
Widowed	—	—
Separated	—	—
Total	**50**	**100.00**

TABLE 7

Age at Marriage

Age	*Frequency*	*Percentage*
15-25	50	100.00
25 and above	—	—
Total	**50**	**100.00**

Family Structure

22 respondents belong to nuclear families while 16 belong to extended families. 12 are from joint families. Family support is necessary for activist women. If there are more members in the family, such women can get reasonable freedom from household duties. Children are well looked after and such women are able to devote more time to their political activities. We all know that the political activities demand too much time and attention. It is slightly surprising that 22 respondents are able to manage political activities living in a nuclear family (Table 8).

TABLE 8

Type of Family of Respondent

Type	*Frequency*	*Percentage*
Nuclear	22	32
Extended	16	32
Joint	12	24
Total	**50**	**100.00**

Economic Activities

Out of the total of Fifty, 42 (84%) respondents are working, 5 are pure housewives (10%) and 3 respondents are students. Among the 42 working women 22 are in some service, 8 are in business. The rest 12 are in agriculture.

Service

12 respondents are in non-gazetted government service while 4 in gazetted government service. Six are working in private services. 2 are in teaching on gazetted post while 12 are on non-gazetted teaching post.

Business

Four respondents are engaged in big business, and the rest four are doing small business.

TABLE 9

Are You Working or are Only Housewife?

Response	*Frequency*	*Percentage*
Working	42	84
Housewife	5	10
Student	3	6
Total	**10**	**100.00**

TABLE 9.1

If Working, State Your Occupation

Service	*N (%)*	*Business*	*N (%)*	*Agriculture*	*N (%)*
Gazetted Govt. Govt. service	4 (18.18)	Big Business	4 (50.00)	Big Agriculture	4
Non Gazetted Govt. Service	12 (54.54)	Small Business	4 (50.00)	Small Agriculture	8
Private Service	6 (27.27)	Others	—	Others	—
Total	**22 (100.00)**	**Total**	**8 (100.00)**	**Total**	**12**

Agriculture

4 are in big agriculture, while 8 are in small agriculture (Table 9).

Monthly Income

24 respondents have a monthly income ranging from Rs. 2000 to Rs 5000, while 23 are earning between Rs. 5000—Rs. 10,000, per month. Three have a monthly income of Rs 10,000 and above (Table 10).

TABLE 10

Monthly Income of Respondent

Response	*Frequency*	*Percentage*
1000 to 2000	—	—
2000 to 5000	24	48
5000 to 10000	23	46
10000 & above	3	6
Total	**50**	**100.00**

Education

49 respondents have varying degrees of education, just one is uneducated. Among the educated 24 are graduate, 5 have master's degree, five have had education up to secondary and three have primary level education. Among the respondents 8 have a Ph.D. degree while 1 is computer educated (Table 11 and 11.1).

TABLE 11

Educational Status of Respondent

Status	*Frequency*	*Percentage*
Educated	49	98
Uneducated	1	2
Total	**50**	**100.00**

TABLE 11.1

If Educated Till Which Level

Level	*N%*	*Technical*	*N%*
Primary	3 (7.5)	B.Ed.	—
Secondary	5(12.5)	Ph.D.	8 (88.89)
B.A.	27 (67.5)	Engg.	—
M.A.	5(12.5)	Management Computer	1(11.1)
Total	**40(100.00)**	**Total**	**9 (100.00)**

Perception of the Self (As Woman)

Thirty-two respondents (645) did not feel that women enjoyed equal status with men while 18 thought that they did. 50 per cent respondents believed in the natural superiority of the males over women. Out of these 25 respondents the reason cited by 15 for the superiority of men over women was due to the prominent place given to them by the society. Ten agreed that the males were physically stronger than women.

Among the 25 respondents who believed that women enjoyed an equal status, 20 maintained that women performed the important job of bringing up the next generation in right direction, while 5 maintained that women performed important social duties as men (Table 12, 13 and 13.1).

TABLE 12

Do You Think that Women Enjoy an Equal States with Men in Real Life?

Response	*Frequency*	*Percentage*
Yes	18	36
No	32	64
Total	**50**	**100.00**

TABLE 13

Do You Think that Men are by Nature Superior to Women?

Response	*Frequency*	*Percentage*
Yes	25	50
No	25	50
Total	**50**	**100.00**

TABLE 13.1

If yes	*N (%)*	*If No*	*N (%)*
They are physically Stronger than women	19 (20%)	Women perform an important duty in society as men	5 (10%)
Society gives them a prominent place	15 (30%)	Women are important for bringing up the next generation in right direction	20 (40%)
Usually they earn better	—	—	—

In response to the question whether women should be educated, all the respondents agreed to it. Thirty (60%) advocated for education upto graduate level, only 6 supported P.G. level education and only 5 were just in favour of secondary education. Nine respondents supported technical education for women. The responses reflect that women do favour education but majority do not link up education with professional and work opportunities. We all know that a mere graduate level education will not enable women to get good jobs (Table 14 and 14.1).

TABLE 14

Should Women be Educated?

Response	*Frequency*	*Percentage*
Yes	50	100
No	—	—
Total	50	

TABLE 14.1

If Yes, Till Which Level?

	Frequency	*Percentage*
Primary	—	—
Secondary	5	10
Graduate	30	60
P.G.	6	12
Technical Education	9	18
Total	**50**	**100.00**

The next Question asked respondents to evaluate the status of educated women vis-a-vis uneducated women 48 (96%) respondents believed that the status of educated women was superior to that of uneducated women (Table 15). This shows that the respondents acknowledge the importance of education for cultivating a positive image and perception of the self.

TABLE 15

Do You Think that the Status of Educated Women in Relation to Uneducated Women is

Response	*Frequency*	*Percentage*
Superior	48	96
Inferior	—	—
Equal	2	4
Total	**50**	**100.00**

Full Time Career

The respondents were asked whether women should have a full time career. Forty-five responded were in favour of full-time career, 20 maintained that it gives economic independence. 13 agreed that it enhances the social status of women while 12 accepted that it gives confidence. The responses reflect that the respondents understand that linkage between economic independence and positive perception of the self. Only 5 have repeated the oft-quoted arguments that economic independence of women leads to family tension and women are not strong enough to cope with full time career physically (Table 16 and 16.1).

TABLE 16

Do You Believe that Women Should have a Full Time Career?

Response	*Frequency*	*Percentage*
Yes	45	90
No	5	10
Total	**50**	**100.00**

TABLE 16.1

If yes, If No

If yes	*N (%)*	*If No*	*N (%)*
It gives confidence	12(26.6)	Economic Independence may break the family	1(20%)
It gives economic independence	20 (44.4)	Temperament and Physical quality may make the job tough	4(80%)
It gives better status in society	13(28.8)	Any other	
Total	**45**	**Total**	**5**

Political Aptitude and Awareness

Accepting the role of aptitude in directing individuals towards particular activities the respondents were served with some questions in order to evaluate their political aptitude.

The respondents were asked whether women should go for full-time political career, and about 30 (60%) approved; 13 strongly and 17 gave simple approval. 14 disapproved of full-time political career, and six disapproved strongly.

Among these who approved 21 reasoned that it will improve the life-conditions of such women while 9 (30%) believed importantly that presence of women will clean politics of corruption.

Among those who disapproved, 16 agreed with the season that politics of the day involves increasing use of money and muscle-power, while 4 thought that women lacked the temperament and physical ability needed for full-time political career (Table 17 and 17.1).

TABLE 17

Would You Approve of Political Career for Women?

Response	*Frequency*	*Percentage*
Strongly approve	13	26
Approve	17	34
Strongly disapprove	6	12
Disapprove	14	28
No opinion	—	—
Total	**50**	**100.00**

TABLE 17.1

If Approve, If Disapprove

If yes	*N (%)*	*If No*	*N (%)*
Entering politics will improve their life condition	21 (70%)	It creates tension in the Family	—
Women's entrance may clean politics	9 (30%)	Damages their image	—
		Lack of temperament and physical ability for tough job	4 (20%)
		It involves a lot of money, increasing use of muscle power	16 (80%)
Total	**30 (100.00)**	**Total**	**20 (100.00)**

Thirty-one (62%) respondents agreed that women could be successful as political leaders and among them 19 reasoned that women have a equal footing with men in this regard and 12 reasoned that our constitution gave equal political rights to women.

Nineteen respondents doubled the success of women as

political leaders. Thirteen thought that women are not able to put in that much of hard work nor they are tough enough to be successful as political leaders. Two maintained that the image and character of such women is tarnished and 4 blamed increasing crime in politics. Obviously these respondents believe that women are not hard working and tough enough to succeed as political leaders. Increasing crime in politics will prevent them to work successfully (Table 18 & 18.1).

TABLE 18

Would Women be Successful in Political Leadership Positions?

Response	*Frequency*	*Percentage*
Yes	31	62
No	19	38
Total	**50**	**100.00**

TABLE 18.1

If yes	*N (%)*	*If No*	*N (%)*
She is an equal footing with men in this regard	19 (61.29)	Lack of social interaction	—
Our constitutes guarantees equal political right to women	12 (38.71)	Lack of hard work and toughness	13 (68.42)
Her achievement in political field itself is her qualification for success		Damaging to image and character	2 (10.52)
		Criminalisation of politics	4 (21.05)
Total	**31 (100.00)**	**Total**	**19 (100.00)**

Political Awareness

The evaluation of political awareness of the respondents in this category is very important because the respondents are political activists. Unless they are aware of the political scenario, their activism will not yield much.

In response to the first question regarding identification of women political leaders from the given list, all the respondents identified Indira Gandhi, and 40 (80%) were able to identify Begum Khalida Zia. Thirty were able to mark Margaret Thatcher, Medha Patkar has been again marked as a politically important women by 35. Most disappointing has been the identification of Mother Teressa as a political women by 7 respondents (Table 19).

TABLE 19

Given Below are Names of Five Important Women Who Among of Them are Politically Important?

If yes	*N*	*%*	*Total*
Mother Teressa	7	14	50
Begum Khalida Zia	40	80	—
Indira Gandhi	50	100	
Margaret Thatcher	30	60	
Medha Patkar	35	70	
Total			

The respondents have not agreed overwhelmingly that Indira Gandhi's position as Prime Minister enhanced the overall status of women. Only 21 (42%) agreed that it has while 29 (58%) did not agree that Indira Gandhi as Prime Minister was able to raise the importance of women. Among those who accepted the influence of Indira Gandhi, 11 maintained that she had become a role-model, 6 accepted that she had defied the myth that women were no good in politics. Four accepted that due to the successful career of Indira Gandhi social attitudes towards women had changed (Table 20 and 20.1).

TABLE 20

Did Indira Gandhi as Prime Minister raise the Overall Status of Indian Women?

Response	*Frequency*	*Percentage*
Yes	21	42
No	29	58
Total	**50**	**100.00**

TABLE 20.1

If Yes, Why

Response	*Frequency*	*Percentage*
She became a role model	11	52.38
Defied the myth that women are no good in politics	6	28.57
Social attitude towards women changed	4	19.05
Total	**21**	**100.00**

After these preliminary questions, the respondents were served with questions to evaluate their awareness of about government pattern, forms, leaders and current political issues:

Forty-one (82%) respondents identified the present Indian Government as Parliamentary while 9 termed it as Presidential. It is a disappointing response from political activists.

All the respondents accepted that Democracy is the most suitable form of Government for India (Table 21 and 21.1).

TABLE 21

What Pattern of Government Does India have at Present?

Pattern of Govt.	*N*	*Percentage*
Parliamentary	41	82
Presidential	9	18
Unitary	—	—
Federal	—	—
Total	**50**	**100.00**

TABLE 21.1

Which Form of Government Do You Consider as More Suitable for India

Response of Govt.	*N*	*Percentage*
Democracy	50	100
Aristocracy	—	—
Dictatorship	—	—
Total	**50**	**100.00**

Political Parties

Fifty respondents named Congress I and Bharatiya Janata Party and Janata Dal as national Parties in India. 48 named CPI and 46 named CPM as National Parties (Table 22).

TABLE 22

Name Five Important Political Parties of National Level

Name of National Parties	*N*	*%*	*Total*
Congress	50	100	50
BJP	50	100	
CPI	48	96	
CPM	46	92	
JD	50	100	

As regards Regional Parties, 45 named Rashtriya Janata Dal while 48 named Telegu Desham and 42 named Jharkhand Mukti Morcha (Table 23).

TABLE 23

Name Five Important Political Parties of Regional Level Including Bihar

Name of Parties	*N*	*%*	*Total*
RJD	45	90	50
JMM	42	84	
Telugu Desham	48	96	
DMK	47	94	
Shiv Sena	41	82	

To cross-check the awareness of respondents regarding parties they were given a mixed list of Political Parties and asked to identify national parties. All the respondents identified Congress I and BJP, while closely identified were Janata Dal (45), CPM (46), Samata Party (48) as national parties. A small number identified RJD and JMM as national parties (Table 24).

TABLE 24

Given Below are Names of Political Parties Which among them are National Parties

Name of Parties	*N*	*%*	*Total*
RJD	2	4	50
Jharkhand Mukti Morcha	6	12	
BJP	50	100	
Samata Party	48	96	
CPI ML	48	96	
Janata Dal	45	90	
D M K	3	6	
Congress I	50	100	
CPM	46	92	
Forward Block	—	—	
Bahujan Samaj Party	—	—	
Jan Mukti Morcha	—	—	

Political Leaders

The respondents were given a mixed list of important men in different fields and were asked to identify political leaders among them. All the Fifty respondents identified Gandhi, Nehru, Lal Bahadur Shastri and Jai Prakash Narain as important political leaders. 43 identified Mao-Tse-Tung as a Political leader (Table 25).

TABLE 25

Given Below the Name of Important Person of the World Who among of them Political Leaders

Name of Person	*N*	*%*	*Total*
Martin Luthar King	8	16	50
Mother Teresa	7	14	
Mahatma Gandhi	50	100	
Karl Marx	11	29	
Swami Vivekanand	—	—	
Jai Prakash Narain	50	100	

Jawahar Lal Nehru	50	100
Mao-Tse-Tung	43	86
Rabindra Nath Tagore	—	—
Lal Bahadur Shastri	50	100
Pandit Ravi Shankar	—	—

Five Women Political Leaders in India

All the fifty respondents named Indira Gandhi, 48 named Sarojini Naidu and Margaret Alva, 47 named Ram Dulari Sinha and 45 named Vijayalakshmi Pandit.

The respondents were given a mixed set of names of women to identify political leaders among them to cross-check their awareness. The name of Indira Gandhi appeared in all the responses while Sarojini Naidu was identified by 48. Medha Patkar was identified by 35 respondents (Table 26 and 27).

TABLE 26

Name Five Important Women in Indian Politics

Name of Women	*N*	*%*	*Total*
Indira Gandhi	50	100	50
Sarojini Naidu	48	96	
Vijay Laxmi Pandit	45	90	
Margaret Alva	48	96	
Ram Dulari Sinha	47	94	

TABLE 27

Given Below are Names of Some Important Women in India Who among them is Political Leader?

Name of Women	*N*	*%*	*Total*
Mahadevi Verma	—	—	50
Medha Patkar	35	70	
M.S. Subhalaxmi	—	—	
Indira Gandhi	50	100	
Sarojini Naidu	48	96	

Bihar

Uma Pandey was named by 48, Tarkeshwari Sinha by 45, Ramdulari Sinha was identified by 47, and Krishna Shahi by 48 Prabhawati Gupta was named by 46. None named Rabri Devi who had become Chief Minister by then (Table 28).

TABLE 28

Name Five Important Women in Politics in Bihar

Name of Women	*N*	%	*Total*
Ramdulari Sinha	47	94	50
Krishna Shahi	48	96	
Prabhawati Gupta	46	92	
Uma Pandey	48	96	
Tarkeshwari Sinha	45	90	

As regards male political leaders from Bihar, very positively Dr. Rajendra Prasad, and Jai Prakash Narain were named by all the respondents. Jagannath Mishra was named by 48, Laloo Prasad Yadav by 47 and Karpoori Thakur by 45 (Table 29).

TABLE 29

Name Five Important Political Leader in Bihar

Name of Leader	*N*	%	*Total*
Dr. Rajendra Prasad	50	100	50
Jai Prakash Narain	50	100	
Karpoori Thakur	45	90	
Laloo Prasad Yadav	47	94	
Dr. Jagannath Mishra	48	96	

Ruling Party

All the respondents identified Rashtriya Janata Dal as the ruling party in Bihar. It is correct in the context of the time when data was collected in the present Government too RJD is the largest segment and the RJD is ruling Bihar with the help and alliance of some other political parties

Bharatiya Janata Dal has been identified by all as the main opposition party in Bihar Vidhan Sabha of the day (Table 30).

TABLE 30

Which Party is Ruling in Bihar at Present (1998-99) and Also Name the Opposition Party

Ruling Party	*N*	*%*	*Opposition Party*	*N*	*%*
RJD	50	100	BJP	50	100
Total	**50**	**100**	**Total**	**50**	**100**

The respondents were asked whether the Government would complete its 5 year term, which it did and once again has came back to power after Vidhan Sabha Elections 2000 (Table 31).

TABLE 31

Do You Think that the Present Government (1998-99) Will Complete Its Five Year Term?

Response	*N*	*%*
Yes	50	100
No	—	—
Total	**50**	**100**

The respondents were asked if they were in favour of a separate Jharkhand State 46 (92%) had disagreed but nevertheless the Jharkhand State did come into existence on 15.11.2000 (Table 32).

TABLE 32

Are You in Favour of a Separate Jharkhand State?

Response	*N*	*%*
Yes	4	8
No	46	92
Total	**50**	**100**

Role of Caste in Bihar Politics

42 respondents agreed to the statement that caste is the bane of politics in Bihar. Among these respondents 28 opined that election on caste line prevented the entry of able and efficient persons in politics, 12 responded that it prevents the Government

from working for the welfare of all. 2 believed that it led to social tensions.

Among the 8 (16%) who disagreed, all believed that it has given the lower and backward castes the chance to enter politics (Table 33 and 33.1).

TABLE 33

Caste is the Bane of Politics in Bihar. Do You Agree?

Response	*N*	%
Yes	42	84
No	8	16
Total	**50**	**100**

TABLE 33.1

If yes	*N (%)*	*If No*	*N (%)*
Voting on Caste basis prohibit able person to come politics	28 (66.67)	It will demolish upper caste hegemony over Bihar Politics	—
It leads to social tensions	2 (4.76)	The backward and lower caste will get a chance to enter politics	8 (100.00)
The Govt. does not work for the welfare of all people	12 (28.57)	It will bring social justice	—
Total	**42 (100.00)**	**Total**	**8 (100.00)**

Evaluation of Bihar Politics

The respondents were asked to evaluate the politics in Bihar 13 (26%) thought it was totally corrupt while 37 did not agree that it was corrupt. As a follow-up the respondents were asked about the characteristics of a good government. 48 placed concern for the welfare of all as the most important mark of a good government. Forty five (90%) pointed to "Stability" as an important mark while 40 favoured a corruption-free Government (Table 34 and 35).

TABLE 34

Do You Agree that Politics in Bihar is Totally Corrupt?

Response	*N*	*%*
Yes	13	26
No	37	74
Total	**50**	**100.00**

TABLE 35

What is Your Opinion Regarding Mark of Good Governments

Response	*N*	*%*	*Total*
Stability	45	90	50
Free of Corruption	40	80	
Concern for the welfare of all the citizen	48	96	
Any other	—	—	

TABLE 36

Are You Active in Politics?

Response	*N*	*%*
Yes	50	100
No	—	—
Total	**50**	**100.00**

Participation in Politics

All the respondents of this category are naturally active in politics. Thirty joined politics in 25-29 years age group. Another 12 joined politics in 30-34 years age-group while six joined in the 35 and above age group just two joined in the younger age group of 20-24 years (Table 36 and 37).

TABLE 37

At What Age Did You Join Politics?

Age of the respondent?	*N*	%
20-24 years	2	4
25-29 years	30	60
30-34 years	12	24
35 & above	6	12
Total	**50**	**100.00**

26 were influenced by their husbands while 13 were influenced by their fathers. So the major influences have been of husband or father. Just 4 decided for themselves (Table 38).

TABLE 38

Who Influenced You to Join Politics?

Who Influenced	*N*	%	*Total*
Father	13	26	50
Mother	2	4	
Brother	1	2	
Sister	—	—	
Friend	3	6	
Husband	26	52	
In-laws	—	—	
Books	—	—	
Speech of Prominent leader	1	2	
Any other (self)	4	8	
Total	**50**	**100.00**	

23 respondents had some family member in active politics. Among these 23, 11 had their fathers in politics, 10 had husbands, just one each had mother and brother in Politics (Table 39 and 39.1).

TABLE 39

Is Any Member of Your Family in Active Politics?

Response	N	%
Yes	23	46
No	27	54
Total	**50**	**100.00**

TABLE 39.1

If Yes What is Your Relation with Her/Him

Relation	N	%
Father	11	17.82
Mother	1	4.35
Brother	1	4.35
Sister	—	—
Husband	10	43.48
Uncle	—	—
Total	**23**	**100.00**

About being acquainted with political literature, 19 did not read such literature, while 31 did. 23 read literature on Democracy while 8 on communism.

TABLE 40

Do You Read Political Literature? If Yes of What Types?

Type of literature	N	%
On democracy	23	46
On Communism	8	16
On Dictatorship	—	—
Do not read	19	38
Total	**50**	**100.00**

Reasons behind reading political literature were given by respondents. 18 liked to read such books, 10 read because they got the books free, 2 were forced by elders while one was forced by party. Among those who did not read such books, ten could not find time for it while 9 did not have any liking for such books (Table 40 and 40.1).

TABLE 40.1

If yes, why	*N (%)*	*If no, why*	*N (%)*
Liking	18 (58.06)	Not permitted by elders	—
Getting free of charge	10 (32.26)	No liking	9 (47.37)
Complied by party	1 (3.22)	Shortage of time	10 (52.63)
Forced by elders	2 (6.44)	Any other	—
Any other	—	—	—
Total	**31 (100.00)**	**Total**	**19 (100.00)**

Attending Political Meetings

About attending political meetings, 32 responded that they did. 19 attended such meetings to know about party programme. Eleven to express their own views (Table 41 and 41.1).

TABLE 41

Do You Attend Political Meetings?

Response	N	%
Yes	32	64
No	18	36
Total	**50**	**100.00**

TABLE 41.1

If Yes on What?

What	N	%
Oratory of the speaker	—	
His/her personality	2	6.25
His/her views	11	34.38
Programme of the party	19	59.37
Any other	—	
Total	**32**	**100.00**

Study Circles

Twenty-three respondents attended study-circles organized by their political parties but 27 did not attend such meetings. Among those who attended, did so to know about party policies, 8 due to the subjects discussed in such study circles and 4 for a desire to know about issues of national and international affairs.

Sixteen among those who did not attend had no liking such meeting and 11 thought it was waste of time (Table 42 and 42.1).

TABLE 42

Do You Attend Study Circles Organized by Any Political Party?

Response	*N*	%
Yes	23	46%
No	27	54%
Total	**50**	**100.00**

TABLE 42.1

If yes, why	*N (%)*	*If no, why*	*N (%)*
Subject discussed	8 (34.78)	Elders not allowing	
Party Politics	11 (47.82)	No liking	16 (59.26)
National and International affairs	4 (17.39)	Waste of time	11 (40.74)
Policies of other parties	—	Fear of being branded as party men	—
Democracy	—	Any other	—
Total	**23 (100.00)**	**Total**	**27 (100.00)**

Participation in Political Activities During Student Days

All the respondents had taken part in political activities during student days.

Sixteen had been members of student's wing of a political party, while 11 were full members of a political party. 17 took part in debates, discussion and symposiums on current political issues. 21 had listened to speeches of important political leaders, while 13 had taken part in rallies. Just 4 used to write on current issues in newspapers and magazines (Table 43).

TABLE 43

Did You Take Part in Any Political Activities in Student Life

Political activities	*N*	*%*	*Total*
Membership of student wing of political party	16	32	50
Taking part in rallies organized by the political parties	13	26	
Listening to speeches of Important political leaders	21	42	
Writing in newspapers or magazines on current political issues	4	8	
Taking part in debates, discussions and symposiums on current political issues	11	22	
Any other	4	8	
Total			

All the respondents are members of some political parties at present. Fourteen, the maximum number in this category belong to CPI ML. Almost equally matching is the number of those respondents (12) who are member of Bharatiya Janata Party. Eight are members of RJD while 5 are associated with JD. Three are members of INC, and two are in CPM. Three are members of Samata Party (Table 44 and 44.1).

TABLE 44

Are You Member of Any Political Party at Present

Response	*Regular Member*	*Active Member*	*Passive Member*
Yes	23 (46%)	10 (82.61)	4 (17.39)
No	27 (54%)	—	—
Total			

TABLE 44.1

If Yes, Name the Party

Name of party	*N*	%
RJD	8	16
Samata	3	6
JD	5	10
CPI ML	14	28
CPM	2	4
IPF	1	2
BJP	12	24
IND	1	2
JMM	1	2
Congress	3	6
Total	**50**	**100.00**

Ten are in the party because they like the party programme. Four have candidly accepted personal benefit as the reason for joining a political party (Table 44.2)

TABLE 44.2

Reason for Membership

Reason	*N*	%
Personal Benefits	4	17.39
Suggested by elders	—	—
Forced by party	2	8.70
Attracted by party Programme	10	43.47
Influenced by the personality of the leader in party	2	8.70
Social Work	5	21.75
Any other	—	—
Total	**23**	**100.00**

Participation in the Activities of Any Political Party

All the respondents are participating in some activity or other of the party they belong 14 are taking part in Morchas, 16 in processions, 18 in demonstrations. Seven Respondents have taken part in Satyagraha. Thirteen have taken part in political movements. The Respondents have taken part in several activities simultaneously (Table 45 and 45.1).

TABLE 45

Do You Take Part in Party Activities?

Response	*N*	%
Yes	50	100
No	—	—
Total	**50**	**100**

TABLE 45.I

What Activities

If yes what activities	*N*	%
Morcha	14	28
Procession	16	32
Demonstration	18	36
Satyagrah	7	14
Political movement	13	26
Any other	4	8
Total	**31**	**100.00**

The respondents were asked about their political aspirations. Nearly 40 (80%) expressed that they had some political aspirations, while 10 did not respond. They were not clear about their aspirations when asked to give details of their aspirations, 20 (40%) replied that they wanted to work for their party. Ten candidly accepted that they wanted to work for the welfare of their caste and 10 admitted that they aspired to get favours from their party leaders (Table 46 and 46.1).

TABLE 46

Do You Have Any Political Aspiration?

Reason	*N*	*%*
Yes	40	80
No Response	10	20
Total	**50**	**100.00**

TABLE 46.1

If Yes

If yes, what?	*N*	*%*
Party work	20	50
Welfare of caste	10	25
Currying favour of party leaders	10	25
Any other	—	—
Total	**40**	**100.00**

Voting Behaviour and Contesting Elections

Part IV B of the schedule sought to persue the voting behaviour of the respondents and their opinion and desire regarding contesting elections. The responses are given below:

Voting

TABLE 47

Voting is Important in Democracy Why?

Reason	*N*	*%*
Democracy is the Govt. of the people, for the people by the people	18	36
Voting indicates people's choice of their representative	16	32
Voting is necessary in indirect Democracy	16	32
Any other	—	—
Total	***50***	***100.00***

In response to the first Question whether voting was important in Democracy, 18 considered it important because Democracy is the Government of the people, for the people and by the people. 16 regarded voting important because people can elect their representatives according to their choice. 16 hit the point that Indirect Democracy cannot operate unless people partake and vote in elections (Table 47).

All the respondents had voted sometime or other. Forty respondents had voted first in Lok Sabha elections while 10 had voted in Assembly elections for the first time (Table 48).

TABLE 48

Have You Voted in Any Election? If Yes, Name Election

Election	*N*	%
Lok Sabha	40	80
Assembly	10	20
Total	**50**	**100.00**

Lok Sabha Elections

One respondent had voted for C.P.I. in 1957. In 1967, 3 had voted one for Congress I and 2 for Jan Sangh. In 1971 on each had voted for Congress and C.P.I. In 1977 one voted for Janata Party and one for Congress I one voted for B.J.P. in 1980, one each for J.M.M. and I.P.F. in 1984, Twelve respondents had voted in 1989, 4 for Congress I, one for J.D., one for Janata Party, 4 for B.J.P. and 2 for I.P.F. Six had voted in 1991—one for C.P.I., 1 for CPI ML, one for J.D., one for B.J.P. and 2 for Congress I. Nine voted in 1996 —one for Samata Party, 1 for C.P.I, and 7 for B.J.P. In 1998 elections two voted for B.J.P. Clearly in the earlier phase the respondents had shown their preference for Congress I, but later B.J.P. has been favoured and support for this party has gradually increased from 1989. Before the emergence of CPI ML, IPF got sizeable preference by voters. Before the emergency of B.J.P., Jan Sangh Party had also attracted the attention of voters (Table 48.1)

TABLE 48.1

Name First Election, Year, and Party Election of Your Voting Lok Sabha

Election	*N (%)*	*Party*
1957	1 (2.5)	CPI
1967	3 (7.5)	Congress, BJP, Jan Sangh
1971	2 (4.00)	Congress, CPI ML
1977	2 (4.00)	Congress, Janta Party
1980	1(1.5)	BJP
1984	2 (4.00)	JMM, IPF
1989	12(30.00)	Congress (4), JD (1), JP (1), BJP (4), IPF (2)
1991	6(15.00)	CPI (1), CPI ML (1), JD (1), BJP (1) Congress (2)
1996	9 (22.5)	Samata (1), CPI(1), BJP(7)
1998	2 (4.00)	BJP (21)
Total	**40 (100.00)**	

Vidhan Sabha

Ten respondents had first voted in Bihar assembly elections. One had voted for CPI in 1962. None among the respondents had voted in 1967 and '69. One had voted for CPI in 1972. Again none voted in 77 and '80 four respondents had voted in 1985, two for Congress and 2 for independent candidates. In 1995, 4 had voted thus—2 for Janata Dal, one for Samata and 1 for Congress I (Table 48.2).

TABLE 48.2

First Voted in Bihar Vidhan Sabha Assembly Elections

Year	*N (%)*	*Party*
1962	1 (10.00)	CPI
1967	—	—
1969	—	—
1972	1 (100.00)	CPI
1977	—	—
1980	—	—

1985	4 (40.00)	Congress (2), IND (2)
1990	—	—
1995	4 (40.00)	JD (2), Samata (1), Congress (1)
Total	**10(100.00)**	

A perusal of the voting Pattern of Political activists shows that they have taken more interest in Lok Sabha elections in comparison to Vidhan Sabha. Out of the total of 50, only 10 had first voted for Vidhan Sabha. No one had voted in the crucial State elections of 1969, 77 and '80. The years 1974 and 1975 had witnessed a massive revolution (Total Revolution) in Bihar which was lethal enough to shake the very foundations of the Congress government led by Indira Gandhi at the Centre. Emergency had to be promulgated in the middle of 1995. Women had participated in large numbers in the Total Revolution, and were totally charged and politically alive and active. Yet they had not taken much interest in elections, not even as Voters. At least this is the picture that emerges from a scan of the responses of the respondents in this sample.

The respondents were asked about '98 Lok Sabha election. 48 (96%) had voted, only 2 had not voted. Out of those who had voted (48), 19 voted for CPI ML, 7 for Congress I, 7 for B.J.P., 2 for Samata, 1 for J.M.M. and one for independent candidate. Five had voted due to the fascinating personality of the candidate, 5 due to the image of the party and 34 had voted on the basis of party programme and party manifesto. Only one admitted to have voted on caste consideration, 2 on the suggestion of some other person and one was forced to vote for a particular candidate (Table 49 and 49.1).

TABLE 49

Were You a Voter in 1998 Lok Sabha Election?

Response	N	%
Yes	48	96
No	2	4
Total	**50**	**100.00**

TABLE 49.1

Name of Party and Reason

Name of the party	*N (%)*	*Reasons*	*N(%)*
Congress	7(14.58)	Fascinating Personality	5(10.41)
CPI ML	18 (37.5)	Party	5(10.41)
JD	11 (22. 91)	Party Programme Manifesto	34 (70.83)
BJP	7(14.58)	Caste	1 (2.08)
Samata	2 (4.16)	Religion	—
JMM	1 (2.08)	Suggested by other	2 (41.6]
IPF	1 (2.08)	Forced by other	1 (2.08)
Independent	1 (2.08)	—	—
Total	**48 (100.00)**		**48 (100.00)**

Assembly Elections '95

45 (90%) had voted in '95 elections while 5 had not. Out of the 45, 18 had voted for CPI ML, 8 for J.D., 7 for B.J.P. and 9 for Congress I. One had voted for Samata, 1 for JMM and 1 for independent candidate.

For 20, the main reason behind their voting was their liking for the particular Party programme. Sixteen voted just in the name of party while 8 were influenced by the personality of the candidate one voted on other person's advice (Table 50 and 50.1).

TABLE 50

Were You a Voter in 1995 Assembly Election in Bihar?

Response	*N*	*%*
Yes	45	90
No	5	10
Total	**50**	**100.00**

TABLE 50.1

Name of Party, Reasons

Name of the party	*N (%)*	*Reasons*	*N(%)*
Congress	9(20%)	Fascinating Personality	8(17.78)
CPI ML	17(37.78)	Party	16(35.55)
JD	8(17.78)	Party Programme	20(44.49)
BJP	17 (15.57)	Religion	—
IPF	1(2.22)	Suggested by other	1(2.22)
Samata	1 (2.22)	—	—
JMM	1 (2.22)	—	—
Independent	1 (2.22)	—	—
Total	**45 (100.00)**	**Total**	**45 (100.00)**

Canvassing for any Party

Out of the total 48 (96%) had canvassed for some Political Party during elections. 28 had canvassed for Lok Sabha elections while 20 had worked for Bihar Vidhan Sabha elections (Table 51).

TABLE 51

Have You Taken Part in Canvassing in Election

Election	N	%
Yes	48	96
No	2	4
Total	**50**	**100.00**

Lok Sabha Elections

In 1977, 7 had canvassed for Janata Party while two for Congress I. In 1980, 2 had canvassed for BJP while 2 had worked for Congress I. In 1984, 2 had canvassed for Congress I while increased to four in '89. One each worked for J.D. in '84 and '87. One canvassed for IPF in '89. Two had worked for BJP in '91, 2 for JD in '96 and 2 for RJD in '98 (Table 51.1).

TABLE 51.1

Canvassing in Lok Sabha Electi .s

Year	*N (%)*	*Party*
1977	2(7.14)	Congress
	7 (25.00)	Janta Party
1980	2(7.14)	BJP
	1 (3.57)	Congress
1984	2(7.14)	Congress
	1 (3.67)	JD
	1 (3.57)	BJP
1989	4(14.28)	BJP
	1 (3.57)	JD
	1 (3.57)	IPF
1991	2(7.14)	BJP
1996	2(7.14)	JD
1998	2(7.14)	RJD
Total	**28(100.00)**	

Assembly Elections

One each had worked for Congress I and Jan Sangh in 1969 while 3 had worked as canvasser for their party in 1972—1 for Jan Sangh and one each for CPI and CPM. In 1977, 4 had worked for Janata Party. In 1980, 2 had worked for BJP and one for IPF. In 1985, 2 had canvassed for JD, one for BJP and one for an Independent candidate. In '90 one had worked for BJP while one had canvassed for independent candidate. In 1995 one had worked for BJP and one for independent candidate (Table 51.2).

TABLE 51.2

Canvassing in Vidhan Sabha Elections

Year	*N (%)*	*Party*
1969	1 (5.00)	Congress
1972	1 (5.00)	Jan Sangh
	1 (5.00)	CPI
	1 (5.00)	CPI ML
1977	4 (20.00)	JP

(Contd.)

(Contd. Table 51.1)

1980	2(10.00	BJP
	1 (5.00)	IPF
1985	2(10.00)	JD
	1 (5.00)	BJP
	1 (5.00)	IND
1990	1 (5.00)	BJP
	1 (5.00)	IND
1995	1 (5.00)	BJP
	1 (5.00)	IND
Total	**20(100.00)**	

Reasons for Canvassing

20 (40%) had canvassed on party programme while 10 were influenced by the personality of the candidate. Ten were related to the candidate. Five did it for personal benefit while five did it just for fun (Table 52).

TABLE 52

Reasons for Canvassing

Reasons	*N*	%
Party Programme	20	40
Personality of the Candidate	10	20
Relation with Candidate	10	20
Religion	—	—
For Fun	5	10
Personal benefit	5	10
Total	**50**	**100**

Canvassing is an important activity during elections, or one can say, immediately before the elections. Much depends on proper canvassing, and women are organized for canvassing. Women activists play an important role as canvassers, and especially Janata Dal and now R.J.D. and CPI ML have been able to mobilize women as canvassers in large numbers. Earlier, the women associated with Congress did a great job as canvassers for their party.

The respondents were tested for their observation of the election scenario. 14 witnessed the operation of caste and communal interests during elections. Thirteen saw "Goonda" elements, 13 witnessed extravagancy of money and 8 were awed with the blatant use of muscle power (Table 53).

TABLE 53

Did You Notice the Following Elements Operating During the Elections?

Elements	N	%
Castism and Communalism	14	28
Goondaism	13	26
Groupism	2	4
Extravagance of money	13	28
Use of muscle power	8	16
Any other	—	—
Total	**50**	**100.00**

Desire to Contest Elections

Thirty-five (70%) respondents desired to contest election When asked about reason, 18 (51.42) desired it to gain power while 11 (31.43) wanted to contest elections and, of course, win to gain social prestige, six desired it for a higher purpose to serve people.

TABLE 54

Do You Desire to Contest Elections?

Response	N	%
Yes	35	70
No	15	30
Total	**50**	**100.00**

Those who did want to enter electoral politics also had their own reason. Out of the 15 (30%) who did not desire to contest elections, 10 (66.67) felt that the political parties were apathetic towards women in giving party ticket. Three (20%) feared increasing violence during the elections while 2 (13.35) admitted that there was lack of funds. It is obvious that those who refrained from contesting elections had very solid reasons—lack of funds, increasing violence and certainty the apathy of political parties towards women. So it was not lack of aptitude or awareness that prevented women. It was very much a result of the situational factors (Table 54 and 54.1).

TABLE 54.1

If Yes, Why? If No, Why?

If yes, why	*N (%)*	*If no, why*	*N (%)*
Desire to serve people	6 (17.14)	Lack of funds	2 (13.33)
For power	18 (51.42)	Apathy of Political Parties in giving ticket	10 (66.67)
For Social Prestige	11 (31.43)	Increasing violence during election	3 (20.00)
Any other	—	Any other	—
Total	**35 (100.00)**	**Total**	**15 (100.00)**

Change of Party Membership

The respondents were asked if they had changed their party any time. 21 (42%) had changed parties while 29 (58%) had remained with the same party. Four (19.54) had changed their party in 1988 from Congress to Janata Dal. Three (14.25) had changed party in 1996 from Janata Dal to Samata Party. Fourteen (51.91) had changed party in 1998. Two left R.J.D. and joined B.J.P. while 4 left B.J.P. to join C.P.I, and 8 left Congress to join R.J.D. (Table 55 and 55.1).

TABLE 55

Here You Changed Your Party Membership

Response	*N*	*%*
Yes	21	42
No	29	58
Total	**50**	**100.00**

TABLE 55.1

If Yes, Name the Year Old Party and New Party

Year	*N (%)*	*Old Party*	*N(%)*	*New Party*	*Reason*	*N (%)*
1988	4 (19.04)	Congress Party	4 (19.04)	JD		
1996	3 (14.29)	Janta Dal	3 (14.29)	Samata		
1998	14 (61.41)	RJD	2 (9.53)	BJP		
		BJP	4 (19.04)	CPI		
		Congress	8 (38.19)	RJD		
Total	**21 (100.00)**		**21 (100.00)**			

The next Question put to them was regarding Anti-defection Law. The respondents were asked to give their opinion on this controversial issue. 32 (64%) approved of this Law while 18 (36%) did not. Among those who supported it, 10 (31.25) believed that it will check opportunism in politics. As we have all been observing in the last one and a half decade, defection at crucial moments has become a common event. Twelve respondents (37.5) expected that party discipline will become more strong. 8 (25%) supported it for the stability of Government while 2 (6.25) thought that it will check corruption.

TABLE 56

Do You Approve Anti-Defection Law?

Response	*N*	*%*
Yes	32	64
No	18	36
Total	**50**	**100.00**

Among the 18 who disapproved, nine (50%) maintained that it will check the arbitrariness of party leadership, seven

(38.39) believed that second rank leaders will get a chance to get higher positions, while 2 (11.10) did not want Anti Defection Law because according to them there will be more democratic functioning of Political Parties (Table 56 and 56.1).

TABLE 56.1

If yes, why	*N (%)*	*If no, why*	*N (%)*
To check opportu-nism in Politics	10 (31.25)	It will check arbitrary-ness of party leaders	9 (50.00)
To develop party discipline	12 (3.75)	Second rank leaders will get a chance to get higher position	7 (38.89)
For stability of Government	8 (25.00)	More democracy within the party	2 (11.10)
To check corruption	2 (6-25)		
Total	**32 (100.00)**	**Total**	**18 (100.00)**

Regarding party support for contesting elections, all the Fifty respondents were in agreement. Twenty-two (44%) regarded party support necessary for publicity of the candidate and his/her party, 14 (28%) maintained that party strength helps, and 18 (36%) said that the party can influence the electorate. Twenty-three (46%) respondents hit the crucial point-that party arrange for funds. Eleven (22%) believed that party provides a platform to the contesting candidate (Table 57 and 57.1).

TABLE 57

Do You Believe that Party Support is Necessary for Contesting Election?

Response	N	%
Yes	50	100
No	—	—
Total	**50**	**100.00**

TABLE 57. 1

If Yes, Reasons

Response	N	%
Party provides a platform	11	22
Gives publicity	22	44
Party strength	14	28
Influences the electorate in favour	18	36
Provides funds	23	46
Any other	—	—

In a nutshell, all the respondents appreciate the role played by the political party. Observation has proved times without number that very few have been able to contest independently and win in the elections. Mostly, the security deposits of Independent candidates are lost, excepting just a few persons who are or have been a political big-wig, or very rich, known and respected in some other field of life.

33% Reservation for Women in Lok Sabha and Vidhan Sabha

The respondents were asked to give their opinion on this burning issue related closely to women. Forty-three (86%) respondents were in favour of reservation for women while seven did not support it.

Table 58

What's Your Reaction to 33% Reservation for Women in Lok Sabha and Assembly?

Response	N	%
Yes	43	86
No	7	14
Total	**50**	**100.00**

TABLE 58.1

If yes, why	*N (%)*	*If no, why*	*N (%)*
It will make ease for women to fight election	14 (32.56)	It is against the Principle of Democracy	—
Parties will be forced to put up women candidates	13 (30.23)	Only elite women will benefit	7 (100.00)
Their present in the Lok Sabha and Vidhan Sabha will be felt	6 (13.95)	Problem of the common women will not be highlighted	
They will bring up the problem in these Sabha and forced remedies	10 (23.25)	It will affect working of the Sabha	
		Because most of the women will be inexperienced	
Total	**43 (100.00)**	**Total**	**7 (100.00)**

Among those who agreed 14 (32.50) reasoned that contesting elections will become easier for women. Thirteen (30.30) had a wishful thinking that parties will be forced to put up more women candidates. Ten expected that women specific issues will be easily brought to the Lok Sabha and Vidhan Sabha. Six (13.95) were of the opinion that if there are more women in these bodies, their presence will be felt in the house.

All the seven who did not support reservation thought that it will benefit only elite women (Table 58 and 58.1).

A detailed interview was taken of some of the prominent activists from the leading political parties to obtain a closer view of their activists their ideas, opinion on important political issues, their aspirations and their struggles.

Sukhada Pandey

Sukhada Pandey has been actively associated with politics since her student days. She was associated with the Jan Sangh

Party as a student member and took part in party activities. She became associated with Bharatiya Janata Party ever since its inception in 1980. She rose to the rank of member of national council of B.J.P. After a gap of one decade she again has become active in politics. Ever since the age of twenty-five she has been active in politics. She has been mostly concerned with the literacy activities of the party, and has also mobilized women. Sukhada Pandey is well known as a very good canvasser and she has actively canvassed for such top leaders as the present Prime Minister, Shri Bajpai. She has been a good and regular voter since 1980 Lok Sabha and Vidhan Sabha Election and has voted for BJP. She has never changed her party. She has a very positive image of women. If men are superior, it is due to importance given to them by society. She advocates full time political career for women She fully supports Anti-Defection Law because it will bring stability, commitment and code of ethics in politics. She also supports 33% reservation for women in Lok Sabha and Vidhan Sabha because the political parties will be under pressure to put up a required number of women candidates. Also, women related problems and issues will be brought into the Lok Sabha and Vidhan Sabha, and if women are present in good number, they can also force the implementation of remedial measures.

Sukhada Pandey is highly educated M.A. and Ph.D in Hindi from Patna University, and has been working in local Magadh Mahila College, Patna University for last 31 years. She is now University Professor and also very active in cultural activities such as debates, symposium, drama etc.

Post Script

Sukhada Pandey won the Bihar Vidhan Sabha Election in 2000 from Buxar and has performed very well as a vocal, articulate and hardworking legislator in Bihar.

Saroj Chaube

Saroj Chaube from CPI ML is a hard-core activist. She has been actively associated with left politics since her student days An M.A. from Allahabad University she was active in progressive students organization and the student union. She came into contact with CPI ML activists and naxal movement. She joined the CPI ML Party in 1986, when the party was underground. She joined active politics in 1990 and worked with Indian People's Front (IPF) Party which was the surface edition of CPI ML. CPI ML came into open in December '92 and IPF was dissolved in 1993. Saroj Chaube was in State Committee in 1973 and was elected to central committee of CPI ML in 1995.

Saroj Chaube takes very active part in mobilizing women, and works with progressive women's Front—the women's wing of the party since 1991. She was state level Secretary. All India Progressive Women's Association was formed in 1994 and Saroj Chaube has been and is the President of AIPWA Bihar branch. She is also the Secretary of APIPWA National level. Saroj Chaube has immense capacity for mobilization and organizing women for their reaction on current political issues which affect all, not only women. She is a well-read person especially of left literature, a severe critic of the present day political leadership at the Centre and Bihar, and has unlimited zeal for placing violence against women and girl child in the fore-front, and involve people for their reaction and their help in solving such issues. She is an activist in true sense of the term. She is fighting fiercely a battle for the dignity and better life conditions of the down-trodden, socially and economically weak masses.

She contested Vidhan Sabha Election from Gaya mufassil in 1995 and Lok Sabha Elections from Patna in 1998 and 1999.

Ms Chaube has not won any election till now which may be due to several reason such as lack of funds, non acceptance of CPI ML ideology by the larger section of people especially in Urban areas, but she is one women who could bring in fresh air in the Vidhan Sabha and bring forward a style of politics which is based on "ideology" and is impregnated with Missionary Zeal.

Bharati S. Kumar

Ms Kumar is a teacher of History in Patna University for nearly three decades. A powerful speaker and articulate in her thoughts, she is actively associated with CPI ML. She is the Vice President of AIPWA, Bihar Branch. She is known for her critical assessment of the political issues. She is specially concerned with increasing violence against women and girl-child and is front rank organizer of demonstrations, protest rallies, dharnas and a very powerful speaker. She can criticize the ruling parties ruthlessly. She is very active in finding remedies for rape-victims. Open in her ideas she is a vocal champion of the dignity, freedom and rights of women.

Ms Bharati joined politics in the tender age of eighteen, and was influenced by her father and later her husband. Her father and husband are associated with politics. She was a member of the student wing of a political party as student, attending meetings, listening to speeches of the leaders and reading political literature. She is a member of CPI ML party and very active. She is mainly attracted by the party program. She has aspiration to be in politics, and she pursues the work of the her party. She has been and is a very good canvasser of CPI ML during elections. She desires to contest elections, but as yet she has not entered electoral politics.

Dr. Kumar is in favour of anti-defection law, and supports 33% reservation for women. Women like Bharati S. Kumar could be an asset to party and could perform very well in Vidhan Sabha as a legislator. Such women should be helped with funds to contest elections. They are not only articulate, dedicated and hardworking themselves, they can and will mobilize and train women for political roles effectively as well.

Phaulen Kuzoor

Ms Kuzoor is an activist associated with Rashtriya Janata Dal. She belongs to the Tribal Community and is placed in Ranchi which is now the capital of newly created Jharkhand State. She was the General Secretary of RJD district council of Ranchi. She is a Christian and is comparatively young -belongs to the age-group of 25-35 years. She is an M.A. and also qualified in NET of the U.G.C. She has a private job. Ms Kuzoor has joined politics at 30 years of age. She was influences by her husband. Her father is in politics. She is closely associated with RJD and attends the meetings and participates in other party activities. Unlike others she was not associated with politics as a student, but she is at present a regular member of RJD. She changed her party from Janata Dal to RJD when the JD split because she has full faith in the leadership of Laloo Prasad Yadav. She has been a regular voter from 1985 onwards. In 1985 she had voted for Congress I but later voted for JD. She desires to contest elections but has not entered electoral politics till now. However she has actively participated in all the party programmes, such as morcha, rally, demonstrations etc.

She is in favour of Anti-Defection Law. If defection is allowed, the defectors betray the trust of their voters.

She supports 33% reservation for women. She believes that if women are present in good number the problems of women will be highlighted in Lok Sabha, Vidhan Sabha, and remedies will be sought with more honestly and measures will be implemented with more integrity.

Aparna Bhattacharya

She is a retired teacher of History from Patna University. She is actively associated with CPM party till today. She, naturally approves of political career for women and believes that women could be successful in leadership positions. Aparnaji joined politics at the age of 30 under the influence of her husband. Her husband and son are active in left politics. She has read political literature, attends political meetings regularly. During her student days, she was a member of the Students Federation of India. She listened to speeches of important political leaders. Presently a member of CPM she has been very attracted to the party programmes. However, she does not have any political aspiration at this stage. She has been engaged in campaigning for CPM in various elections. She does desire to contest elections for serving people.

She supports Anti-Defection Law, because in her opinion the defectors violate the trust of their voters. She supports 33% reservation for women, because if there are more women in Lok Sabha/Vidhan Sabha, the problems of women will be placed on the table and discussed. Efforts will be made to devise strategies for solving the issues.

The respondents in this category are much more aware politically than the earlier category of "professionals" and housewives. They have experience of working in and for Political

Parties. They had played an important role in canvassing for the Party Candidates and have especially been able to mobilize women voters. Most of them are reasonably educated and work accordingly to an agenda placed before them. They have taken part in the various party activities, regularly and one among them has been able to successfully win the Vidhan Sabha (Bihar) elections in 2000. There is a very 'thin' line separating activists from those who are holding positions in political bodies. Most of the activists do desire to enter electoral politics and given chance, may emerge successful and take their place in Vidhan Sabha/Lok Sabha.

6

Women Contestants Who Never Won

This chapter reflects and analyses the responses of the category of women who fought but never won any election. It will help us in ascertaining why women loose elections? What are the factors responsible for their electoral debacle and importantly, what sort of women loose elections? Are they novices in the field of politics, or are fighting elections in dependently without any party support? Are they hardcore activists and have yet lost because they belong to extreme left Parties and/ or do not have enough financial support? Are they just relatives of some political leaders, and were put up as candidates to fill up the vacancy caused by death or some other reason? These are some of the pertinent questions.

This category consists of women ranging from hard-core grass-root activists to total novices. It is an interesting feature of the present political scenario in Bihar and even at the national level that while women who have been persistently working in Political arena have lost while a complete novice wins by a thumping majority, knowing not even the a, b, c of public and political arena, because she is the wife or daughter or widow of some very important political leader.

The aim of selecting such women who never won elections is not to support the oft-quoted and 'mythical' notion that women are a 'liability' because their chances of winning elections are always thin. The election data of recent decades has dispelled this 'myth' and proved that the percentage of women winning elections is higher in relation to the total number of women contestants than the ratio of success of male winners to total male contestants. The aim is to find out why very active "political women" have never been able to win elections. How the situation can be remedied and changed for such deserving women—women who after entering the Lok Sabha or Vidhan Sabha could bring issues of women to the 'centre stage' of the House. Their presence could even help change the political culture of such institutions considerably.

Socio-Economic and Cultural Background of the Respondents

Under 'Social' factors such as religion, caste and sub-castes, marital status family structure and age have been considered.

Religion

Religion—48 (96%) respondents are Hindus while 2 are Christians (Table 1).

TABLE 1

Religion of Respondent

Religion	*N*	*%*
Hindu	48	96
Muslim	—	—
Sikh	—	—
Christian	2	4
Total	**50**	**100**

The Hindu respondents have been put into three categories of castes plus the scheduled tribes for the purpose of record, convenience in analysis. They are:

1. Upper Castes (Brahmin, Rajput, Bhumihar, Kayastha)
2. Backward Castes (Yadav, Kurmi, Baniya and others)
3. Scheduled Castes (Musahar, Dusadh, Chamar, Dhobi, Pasi, Dom)
4. The Scheduled Tribes category includes Bheel, Munda, Santhal and others.

Upper Caste

Out of 50, the upper caste respondents number 16 further subdivided into Brahmines 2, Rajput 5, Bhumihar 4 and Kayastha 5.

Backward Caste

Total number of respondents is 25 further divided thus Yadav 5, Kurmi 5, Baniya 6 and Others 9.

Scheduled Caste

There are six respondents in this category, further divided into Dusadh 2, Musahar 1 and Dhobi, Pasi and Dom one each.

TABLE 2

Caste of Respondent

Caste	*Frequency*	*%*
Upper Caste	16	32
Backward Caste	25	50
S.C.	6	12
S.T.	3	6
Total	**50**	**100.00**

TABLE 2.1

Sub-caste of Respondent

Upper Caste	*N(%)*	*B.C.*	*N(%)*	*S.C.*	*N(%)*	*S.T.*	*N(%)*
Brahman	2 (12.5)	Yadav	5 (20%)	Musahar	1 (16.66)	Bhil	—
Rajput	5 (31.25)	Kurmi	5 (20%)	Dusadh	2 (33.33)	Munda	2 (66.67)
Bhumihar	4 (25%)	Baniya	6 (24%)	Chamar	—	Santhal	1 (33.33)
Kayastha	5 (31.25)	Other	9 (36%)	Dhobi, Pasi, Dom	3 (50%)	Other	—
Total	**16 (100.00)**	**Total**	**25 (100.00)**	**Total**	**6 (100.00)**	**Total**	**3 (100.00)**

In the Scheduled Tribe category there are 2 from Munda Tribe and one is a Santhal (Tables 2 and 2.1).

Age of the Respondents

Eleven respondents belong to the age-group of 25-35 years, 28 belong to 35-50 age group, 10 are from above 50 age group while only one is from 18-25 age group (Table 3).

TABLE 3

Age of Respondent

Age group	*Frequency*	%
18-25	1	2
25-35	11	22
35-50	28	56
50 & above	10	20
Total	**50**	**100**

Place of Birth

32 (64%) were born in villages while 14 (28%) in towns and only 4 (8%) in cities. 26 (52%) spent their early life in towns, 9 in cities and 15 in villages. At present 28 (56%) are living in towns, 15 (30%) in cities and just 7 (14%) in villages (Table 4).

TABLE 4

Place of Birth, Lived Most Early Life, and Live at Present

Place	*Birth*	*Live most early life*	*Live at present*
Village	32 (64%)	15 (30%)	7 (14%)
Town	14 (28%)	26 (52%)	28 (56%)
City	4 (8%)	9 (18%)	15 (30%)
Total	**50 (100.00)**	**50 (100.00)**	**50 (100.00)**

Present Marital Status and Age at Marriage

Out of the total of 50, 48 (96%) are married and just two are unmarried. 49 (98%) were married in the age-group of 15-25 years, and one was married in the above 25 age-group (Tables 5 and 5.1).

TABLE 5

Present Marital Status of Respondent

Status	*Frequency*	%
Married	48	96
Unmarried	2	4
Divorced	—	—
Widowed	—	—
Separate	—	—
Total	**50**	**100.00**

TABLE 5.1

Age at Marriage of Respondent

Age of marriage	*Frequency*	%
15-25	49	98
25 & above	1	2
Total	**50**	**100.00**

Type of Family Structure

19 live in joint families and 18 have nuclear families 13 respondents live in extended families. Taken together 32 (64%) respondents belong to some sort of joint family structure (Table 6).

TABLE 6

Type of Family of Respondent

Type	*Frequency*	%
Nuclear	18	36
Extended	13	26
Joint	19	38
Total	**50**	**100**

Education

All the respondents are educated and among them 27 (54%) are graduates, 13 have had education upto Secondary level, 2 till Primary level and 4 have masters degree, 4 respondents have received technical/ professional education. One has a post-doctoral degree, while three have B.Ed. degree. None of the respondents has had engineering, medical or management education (Table 7 and 7.1).

TABLE 7

Educational Status of Respondent

Status	*Frequency*	*%*
Educated	50	100
Uneducated	—	—
Total	**50**	**100**

TABLE 7.1

Educational Status

Level of education	*N (%)*	*Technical education*	*N (%)*
Primary	2 (4.34)	B.Ed.	3 (75.00)
Secondary	13 (28.26)	Ph.D.	1 (26.00)
B.A.	27 (58.69)	Engg.	—
M.A.	4 (8.69)	Management	—
Total	**46 (100.00)**	**Total**	**4 (100.00)**

Economic Background Working Status of Respondents

47 (94%) respondents are working while 3 are purely housewives. Among those who are working 13 are in government, while 17 are working in non-governmental organizations. One respondent is in Gazetted service while 12 are on non-gazetted posts. In all 30 respondents are in some sort of service.

14 respondents are engaged in Business. Only 4 are working in big business, 6 are in small business and 4 are working full time in Politics. 6 respondents are engaged in agricultural works 4 respondents are in small agricultural jobs while 2 are in big agriculture.

TABLE 9

Monthly Income of Respondent

Monthly Income	*Frequency*	%
1000-2000	—	4
2000-5000	43	86
5000-10000	3	6
10000 & above	2	4
Total	**30**	**100.00**

Perception of the Self as Women

As discussed in the previous chapter, perception of the self, to a great extent, shapes the behaviour, inclinations and goals of life of the individuals. Perception is to a great extent related to the category or group in society an individual belongs to. In almost all societies the norms and traditions assign women to a secondary status as a group which is nonproductive, unambitious and submissive to the male partners. Women are not seen as achievers, creators, inventors but to carry out the established social norms and traditions. Thus there is an inherent feeling of inferiority to and inequality with men, nourished through socialization process since centuries in every society. Universal education, professionalism, urbanization have changed things and thinking to some extent but it is still very persistent. Perceiving oneself as inferior, dependent, non-achiever is bad news for active political career, and one of the main reason women are seen as 'unfit' for political career. This section tries to analyse the responses of the respondents as regards their perception of the self (read women). Forty respondents opine that they do not perceive women enjoying an status equal with men. Only 10 believe that women enjoy equal status with men. Seventeen believe that men are by nature superior to women while encouragingly 33 do not believe in the natural superiority of men. Among the 17 who believe in the natural superiority of men, 13 believe that it is the society that gives them their prominence while 3 regard them as physically superior to women. Among the 33 who disagree, 22 regard women important as they bring up the next generation in right direction. 11 opine that women perform equally important social duties as men (Tables 10, 11 and 11.1).

TABLE 10

Do You Think that Women Enjoy an Equal Status with Men in Real Life

Response	*Frequency*	%
Yes	10	20
No	40	80
N.R.	—	—
Total	**50**	**100**

TABLE 11

Do You Believe that Men are by Nature Superior to Women?

Response	N	%
Yes	17	34
No	33	66
N.R.	—	—
Total	**50**	**100%**

TABLE 11.1

If Yes, If No

If Yes	*N (%)*	*If No*	*N (%)*
They are physically stronger than women	3 (17.64)	Women perform an important duty in society as man	11 (33.33)
Society gives them a prominent place	13 (76.47)	Women are important for bringing up the next generation in right direction	22 (66.67)

Usually they earn Better	1 (5.88)	—	—
Total	**17 (100.00)**	**Total**	**33 (100.00)**

Recognising the role of education for enhancement of the individual image, the respondents were asked whether all women should be educated? The response was overwhelmingly *'yes'*. However majority (29) advocated for graduate level education (the highest for them). 10 supported technical education for women while 9 supported M.A. level education. Only 2 respondents advocated secondary level education (Table 12 and 12.1).

TABLE 12

Should Women be Educated?

Response	*Frequency*	%
Yes	50	100
No	—	—
Total	**50**	**100**

TABLE 12.1

If Yes, Till Which Level?

Which level	*Frequency*	%
Primary	—	—
Secondary	2	4
B.A.	29	58
M.A.	9	18
Technical education	10	20
Total	**50**	**100**

The respondents were asked to give their opinion on the relative superiority of educated women to uneducated women. Happily all the respondents accepted that the status of educated women was superior to uneducated women (Table 13).

TABLE 13

Do You Think that the Status of Educated Women in Relation do Uneducated Women is

	Frequency	%
Superior	50	100
Inferior	—	—
Equal	—	—
No, opinion	—	—
Total	**50**	**100**

Regarding full time career for women which is an important point of perception towards political participation, 29 (58%) respondents were in favour, while 21 (42%) were against it.

Among the 29 in favour, 16 agreed to the fact that it gave economic independence, 7 are of the view that it enhanced their social status while 6 placed their finger on the "nerve" that it generated self-confidence.

TABLE 14

Do You Believes in Full Time Career for Women?

Response	*Frequency*	%
Yes	29	58
No	21	42
N.R:	—	—
Total	**50**	**100**

Among the 21, 14 repeated the oft quoted idea that women would find it 'tough' because of their temperament and physical frailty. 7 feared that economic independence of the women may lead to the break-up of the family (Table 14 and 14.1).

TABLE 14.1

If Yes, why	*N (%)*	*If No, why*	*N (%)*
It gives confidence	6 (20.69)	Económic independence may break the family	7 (33.33)

(Contd.)

(Contd. Table 14.1)

It gives economic Independence	16 (55.17)	Temperament and physical ability may make the job tough	14 (66.67)
It give better status in society	7 (24.14)	Any other	—
Total	**29 (100.00)**	**Total**	**21 (100.00)**

Political Aptitude

It is normally argued that women do not have any aptitude towards 'Politics'. It is a field which is outside their thinking, imagination and aspiration. Yet over the time there has been a change in attitude to some extent. Since we are talking about the category of women who are very much associated with Politics, the responses were expected to reflect the new 'wave' of change.

As regards approval/disapproval of political career for women, a large majority of (42) respondents were found to favour political career for women. Six (12%) gave strong approval for the same while only 2 (4%) disapproved of it. This reflected a significant attitudinal swing towards an acceptance of women's entry in Politics.

Among those who approved, 45 opined that it would cleanse politics of corruption while three opined that women would be able to improve their own life-conditions. Of those who disapproved, both believed that it will create tension in the family (Table 15 and 15.1).

TABLE 15

Approve of Political Career for Women

	Frequency	%
Strongly approve	6	12
Approve	42	84
Strongly Disapprove	—	—
Disapprove	2	4
No opinion	—	—
Total	**50**	**100**

TABLE 15.1

If approve	*N (%)*	*If disapprove*	*N (%)*
Entering politics will improve their life condition	3 (6.25)	It creates tension in family	2 (100%)
Women's entrance may cleanse politics	45 (93.75)	Damages their image	—
—	—	Lack of temperament and physical ability for tough job	—
—	—	It involves a lot of money increasing use of muscle power in politics	–
—	—	Any other	—
Total	**48 (100.00)**	**Total**	**2 (100.00)**

Forty-four respondents (88%) agreed that women would be successful in political leadership positions.

Among them 38 (86.36) opined that the constitution had already provided equal political rights to men and women, 4 (9.09) thought that both men and women are on an equal footing while 2 opined that her achievements in political life will ensure her success. Six (12%) did not believe that women would be successful political leaders because they lacked in doing hard work and also toughness was not their quality (Table 16 and 16.1).

TABLE 16

Would Women be Successful in Political Leadership Positions?

Response	*N*	%
Yes	44	88
No	6	12
Total	**50**	**100**

TABLE 16.I

If Yes	*N (%)*	*If No*	*N (%)*
She is on equal footing with men in this regard	4 (9.09%)	Lack of social Interaction	—
Our constitution guarantees equal political right to men and women	38 (86.36)	Lack of hard work and taughness	6 (100%)
Her achievement in political field itself is her qualification for success	2 (4.54)	Damaging to image and character	—
—	—	Criminalisation of politics	—
Total	**44 (100.00)**	**Total**	**6 (100.00)**

The responses reflect that this category of women by and large had positive aptitude towards politics.

Political Awareness

Realising that awareness was the pre-condition for action or activity, the respondents were given a set of questions in order to test their awareness of matters "political", such as awareness about Forms of government, political theories and ideologies, political leaders, current political issues etc.

TABLE 17

Given Below are Names of Five Important Women Who among them are Politically Important?

Name of Women	*N*	*%*	*Total*
Mother Teressa	4	8	50
Begum Khalida Zia	38	76	50
Indira Gandhi	50	100	50
Margaret Thatcher	45	90	50
Medha Patekar	48	96	50

Identification of political leaders by the respondents is the primary item regarding political awareness. All the respondents recognized Indira Gandhi, while 38 identified Begum Khalida Zia, 45 knew Margaret Thatcher. One surprise response was regarding Medha Patekar being perceived as a political leader by 48 respondents (Table 17).

The respondents were asked whether the position of Indira Gandhi as Prime Minister bring an overall change in the status of women in India? 35 (70%) respondents agreed while 15 (30%) did not. Among the 35 respondents 13 (37.14) maintained that Mrs. Gandhi defied the myth that women were "no good in politics". 19 (54.29) opined that social attitude towards women changed and 3 saw her as a role-model for women. Thus the respondents by and large agreed that the position of Indira Gandhi did bring some change (Table 18 and 18.1).

TABLE 18

Did Indira Gandhi as Prime Minister Raise the Overall Status of Indian Women?

Response	*N*	*%*
Yes	35	70
No	15	30
Total	**50**	**100**

TABLE 18.1

Response	*N*	*%*
She became a role model	3	8.57
Defied the myth that women are no good in politics	13	37.14
Social attitude towards women changed	19	54.29
Total	**35**	**100.00**

Identifying the present form of Government in India, 30 (60%) respondents regarded it to be 'Parliamentary', 17 (34%) respondents wrongly identified it as "Presidential" while three considered it to be Federal. The response was disappointing, because it came from women who had fought elections (Table 19).

TABLE 19

What Pattern of Govt. Does India have at Present?

Pattern	*N*	*%*
Parliamentary	30	60
Presidential	17	34
Unitary	—	—
Federal	3	6
Total	**50**	**100**

All the Respondents agreed that 'Democracy' was the most suitable form of Government for India.

TABLE 20

Which Form of Govt. Do You Consider to be More Suitable for India?

Response	*N*	*%*
Democracy	50	100
Aristocracy	—	—
Dictatorship	—	—
Total	**50**	**100**

TABLE 21

Name Five Important Political Parties of National Level

Name of parties	*N*	*%*	*Total*
Congress	50	100	50
BJP	50	100	50
Janata Dal	48	96	50
CPI	43	86	50
CPM	47	94	50

Regarding National Parties, the response named Congress I and Bharatiya Janta Party. All the respondents named these two parties while 48 named Janata Dal, 43-CPI, 47-CPM as National Parties (Table 21).

Regional Parties— Rashtriya Janata Dal was named by all the respondent, 48 named Jharkhand Mukti Morcha while 46 named Telegu Desham (Table 22).

TABLE 22

Name Five Important Political Parties of Regional Level Including Bihar

Name of parties	N	%	*Total*
RJD	50	100	50
JMM	48	96	50
Telegu Desham	46	92	50
DMK	42	84	50
Shiv Sena	37	74	50

For cross-checking their awareness the respondents were given a set of mixed names of national and regional political parties to identify National Parties. The Congress I and BJP were identified by all, while CPI by 43, Janata Dal by 48, and CPM by 47 (Table 23).

TABLE 23

Below are the Name of Political Parties, Tick the National Parties

Name of parties	N	%	*Total*
RJD	—	—	—
JMM	—	—	—
BSP	4	8	50
BJP	50	100	50
Samata Party	10	20	50
CPI	43	86	50
JD	48	96	50
DMK	2	4	50
Congress	50	100	50
CPM	47	94	50
Forward Bloc	5	10	50
Jan Mukti Morcha	2	4	50

A set of names of important world leaders was given to them to identify among them the political leaders Mahatma Gandhi, Pt. Jawahar Lal Nehru, Jai Prakash Narain, Mao-Tse-Tung and Lal Bahadur Shastri were identified by all as important political leaders (Table 24).

TABLE 24

Given Below are Names of Important Leaders of the World Who among them Were Political Leaders?

Name of Person	*N*	*%*	*Total*
Martin Luthar King	4	8	50
Mother Teressa	2	4	50
Mahatma Gandhi	50	100	50
Karl Marx	4	8	50
Swami Vivekanand	—	—	—
Jai Prakash Narain	50	100	50
Pt. Jawahar Lal Nehru	50	100	50
Mao-Tse-Tung	50	100	50
Rabindra Nath Thakur	—	—	—
Lal Bahadur Shastri	50	100	50
Pandit Ravi Shankar	—	—	—

The respondents were asked to name five important women in Indian Politics. Indira Gandhi, Sarojini Naidu and Margaret Alva were named by all, while 49 (98.0) named Sucheta Kriplani and 48 (96.0) named Vijayalaxmi Pandit. The response was not very satisfactory. Not a single political leader of the present day either from Janata Dal, Congress I, BJP or the Left Parties was named by the respondents (Table 25).

TABLE 25

Name Five Important Women in Indian Politics

Name	*N*	*%*	*Total*
Indira Gandhi	50	100	50
Sarojini Naidu	50	100	50
Sucheta Kriplani	49	98	50
Vijayalaxmi Pandit	48	96	50
Margaret Alva	50	100	50

To cross-check their awareness, the respondents were served with a set of names of important women in different spheres, and were asked to identify political leaders among them. The names identified by all were Indira Gandhi, Sarojini Naidu and Medha Patekar (Table 26).

TABLE 26

Given Below are Name of Important Women of India, Who among them is a Political Leader?

Name of women	*N*	*%*	*Total*
Mahadevi Verma	—	—	50
Medha Patekar	50	100	
M.S. Subhlaxmi	—	—	
Indira Gandhi	50	100	
Sarojini Naidu	50	100	

Bihar

The respondents were asked to name five important women politicians in Bihar. Thirty-five named Rabri Devi (She being the Chief Minister since '97 August). Kanti Singh was named by 42, while Krishna Shahi, Uma Pandey and Tarkeshwari Sinha were named by all the respondents.

The respondents were asked to name five important political leaders of Bihar. All the respondents named Dr. Rajendra Prasad, Jai Prakash Narain, Jagannath Mishra, 48 named Ram Vilas Paswan while 43 named Laloo Prasad Yadav. The response was more or less accurate (Table 27 and 28).

TABLE 27

Name Five Important Women in Politics in Bihar

Name	*N*	*%*	*Total*
Rabri Devi	35	70	50
Kanti Singh	42	84	
Krishna Shahi	50	100	
Uma Pandey	50	100	
Tarkeshwari Sinha	50	100	

TABLE 28

Name Five Important Political Leader in Bihar

Name	*N*	*%*	*Total*
Laloo Prasad Yadav	43	86	50
Ram Vilas Paswan	48	96	
Jai Prakash Narain	50	100	
Dr. Rajendra Prasad	50	100	
Jagannath Mishra	50	100	

All the respondents correctly identified the Rashtriya Janta Dal as the ruling party in Bihar. The data was collected in '98 and '99. Things have changed with 2000 elections when a government had to be formed with the help of Congress I among other segments. Nevertheless R.J.D. is still the largest segment of the ruling alliance. The respondents have correctly identified Bharatiya Janata Party as the opposition party in Bihar (Table 29).

TABLE 29

Name the Ruling Party (Till Mid '99) in Bihar and Opposition Party in Bihar

Name of Ruling Party	*Yes*	*No*	*Total*
Rashtriya Janata Dal	50(100%)	—	50
Name of Opposition Party			
Bharatiya Janata Party	50(100%)	—	50

The respondents were asked whether government of the day would complete its term of office. As we have seen it has. However at the time of data collection 8 respondents were doubtful if the government would complete its term (Table 30).

TABLE 30

Do You Think that the Present Govt. Will Complete Its Five Year Term?

Response	*N*	*%*
Yes	42	84
No	8	16
Total	**50**	**100**

The respondents were also asked to give their opinion on the creation of a separate Jharkhand State. Only 13 respondents were in support while 37 were against its creation. However, a separate Jharkhand State did come into existence on 15.11.2000 (Table 31).

TABLE 31

Are You in Favour of a Separate Jharkhand State?

Response	N	%
Yes	13	26
No	37	74
Total	**50**	**100**

TABLE 32

Caste is the Bane of Politics in Bihar Do You Agree?

Response	N	%
Yes	33	66
No	17	34
Total	**50**	**100**

TABLE 32.1

If Yes, why	N (%)	*If No, why*	N (%)
Voting on caste lines prohibits able person entry into politics	19 (57.57)	It will demolish upper caste hegemony on Bihar Politics	7 (41.18)
It leads to social tensions	8 (24.24)	The backward and lower caste will get a chance to enter politics	10 (58.82)
The Govt. does not work for the welfare of all people	6 (18.18)	It will bring social justice	—
Total	**33 (100.00)**	**Total**	**17**

The respondents were asked to opine whether caste was the 'Bane' of politics in Bihar. 33 responded 'yes' while 17 were against it. Among 33, 19 believed that castism in prevents able persons from joining politics. Eight opined that caste-based politics leads to social tensions (which is amply visible in Bihar's political scenario) and 6 maintained that such a government does not keep in mind the welfare of all the people. Among the 17 who favoured caste based present politics in Bihar, seven (41.18) were hopeful that the upper caste hegemony over politics in Bihar will be demolished, ten (58.82) thought that the backward and lower caste people will get a chance to do well in politics (Table 32 and 32.1).

Surprisingly, only 11 respondents accepted that Politics in Bihar is totally corrupt. The rest 39 respondents did not respond in favour (Table 33).

TABLE 33

Do You Agree that Politics in Bihar is Totally Corrupt?

Response	*N*	%
Yes	11	22
No	39	78
Total	**50**	**100**

The respondents were asked to identify the characteristics of a good government. 40 responded in favour of stability, 42 regarded concern for the welfare of all as a necessary mark while 35 believed that absence of corruption is the mark of a good government (Table 34).

TABLE 34

In Your Opinion, What is the Mark of Good Government?

Mark of Good Govt.	*N*	%	*Total*
Stability	40	80	50
Free of Corruption	35	70	
Concern for the Welfare of all the Citizen	42	84	
Any other	—	—	
Total			

Participation in Politics

Regarding their participation in Politics we find that all the 50 respondents were active in Politics. 44 joined politics in the age-group of 25-35 years while four joined in the age-group of 15-24 years. Only two joined politics after 35 years of age. The main influence for 24 was of their fathers while 16 were influenced by their husbands. In the case of 4, it was the influence of their mother while for three brothers exerted their influence.

Forty-nine respondents had some family member active in family. The maximum 44 had their husbands in active politics. Fathers and brothers of two each respondents were in Politics (Table 35, 36, 37, 38 and 38.1)

TABLE 35

Are You Active is Politics?

Response	*Frequency*	*%*
Yes	50	100
No	—	—
Total	**50**	**100**

TABLE 36

Age of Joining Politics

Age Group	*Frequency*	*%*
18 -24	4	8
25-35	44	88
36-50	2	4
Total	**50**	**100**

TABLE 37

Who Influenced You to Join Politics?

Person	N	%
Father	24	48
Mother	4	8
Brother	3	6

(Contd.)

(Contd. Table 37)

Sister	1	2
Friend	1	2
Husband	16	32
In-laws	—	—
Books	—	—
Speech of prominent leaders	—	—
Any other (self)	1	2
Total	**50**	**100**

TABLE 38

Is Any Number of Your Family in Active Politics?

	N	%
Yes	49	98
No	1	2
Total	**50**	**100**

TABLE 38.1

If Yes, What is Your Relation with Her/Him?

Relation	*N*	%
Father	2	4.8
Mother	—	—
Brother	2	4.08
Husband	44	80.79
Uncle	1	2.05
Total	**49**	**100.00**

TABLE 39

Do You Read Political Literature?

Response	*N*	%
Yes	48	96
No	2	4
Total	**50**	**100**

For Political awareness, the study of political literature is important 48 (96%) respondents did read political literature, 40 on Democracy. Out of these 48, 40 liked to read such literature, 6 were compelled by their party. The two who did not read such literature, did so because of shortage of time (Table 39, 39.1 and 39-2).

TABLE 39.1

If Yes, What Type?

Type of Literature	*N*	*%*
On democracy	40	83.33
On communism	—	—
On dictatorship	—	—
Any other	8	16.67
Total	**48**	**100.00**

TABLE 39.2

If Yes, reason	*N (%)*	*If No, reason*	*N (%)*
Liking	40 (83.33)	Not permitted by elders	—
Getting free of charge	1 (2.08)	No liking	—
Compelled by party	6 (12.5)	Shortage of time	2 (100%)
Forced by elders	—	Any other	—
Any other	1 (2.08)	—	—
Total	**48 (100.00)**	**Total**	**2 (100.00)**

Attending Political Meeting and Party Study Circle

44 respondents did attend political meetings out of which 18 did so because they liked the speech of the speaker, 11 because of their views, and 13 to know about their party programme (Table 40 and 40.1).

TABLE 40

Do You Attend Political Meetings?

Response	N	%
Yes	44	88
No	6	12
Total	**50**	**100**

TABLE 40.1

If Yes, on What

Response	N	%
Oratory of the speaker	18	40.9
His/her personality	2	4.5
His/her views	11	25
Programme of the party	13	29.5
Any other	—	—
Total	**44**	**100.00**

44 attended study-circles out of which 40 attended because of the issues discussed therein, 42 to know about party politics, 35 to knew about national and international issues, 38 wanted to know about Democracy while 14 went to get an idea about the policies of other parties.

4 out of those who did not attend regarded it as waste of time and 2 had no liking for it (Table 41 and 41.1).

TABLE 41

Do You Attend Study Circles Organized by Any Political Party?

Response	N	%
Yes	74	88
No	6	12
Total	**50**	**100**

TABLE 41.1

If yes, why	N (%)	*If No, why*	N (%)
Name of the parties	-	Elders not allowing	—
Subject discussed	40 (90.91)	No liking	2 (33.33)
Party politics	42 (95.45)	Waste of time	4 (66.67)
National and International Affairs	35 (79.45)	Fear of being branded as party man	—
Policies of other parties	14 (31.81)	Any other	—
Democracy	38 (86.36)	—	—
Dictatorship	—	—	—
Total	**44 (100.00)**	**Total**	**6 (100.00)**

TABLE 41.2

Name of Party

Name	N	%
Congress	5	11.36
BJP	3	6.89
JD	12	27.22
RJD	11	25.00
BSP	3	6.89
Samata Party	4	9.09
IPF	1	2.27
BPP	1	2.27
Shiv Sena	1	2.27
CPI	3	6.89
PPM	44	100.00

Among those who attended party meetings and study circles, 5 belonged to Congress I, 3 to BJP, 12 to JD, 11 to RJD, 3 to BSP, 4 to Samata Party, 1 to CPI ML, 1 to BPP, 1 to Shiv Sena and 3 to CPI (Table 41.2).

Student day political activities— 34 respondents had been members of student's wing of a political party. 14 took part in rallies organised by Political Parties 36 respondents listened to the speeches of important political leaders. Sixteen took part in debates, discussions and symposiums organized by their party while 6 wrote on current political issues in newspapers and magazines 4 were full members of the political parties of their choice (Table 42).

TABLE 42

Did You Take Part in Any of the Political Activities in Student Days?

Political activities	N	%
Membership of student wing of political party	34	68
Taken part in rallies organized by the political parties	14	28
Listening to speeches of important political leaders	38	76
Writing in newspapers and magazines on current political issues	6	12
Taking part in debates, discussions and symposiums on current political issues	16	32
Full fledged membership of any political party		
Any other	2	4

As far as Membership of Political Parties at present, we find that forty respondents were regular members of Political Parties. Thirty-five accepted that they were active members.

TABLE 43

Are You Regular Member of Any Political Party at Present

	N	%
Yes	40	80
No	10	20
Total	**50**	**100**

Maximum (11) belonged to RJD, 5 to Congress I, 3 to BJP, 2

to JD, 4 to Samta Party, 3 to CPI and 4 to CPM. Three belonged to BSP, and three to BPP and 2 to JMM (Table 43, 43.1 and 32.2).

TABLE 43.1 AND 43.2

If Yes

Name of party	*N(%)*	*Are active or passive member?*	*N(%)*
Congress	5 (12.5)	Active	35 (75%)
BJP	3 (7.5)	Passive	5 (25%)
RJD	11 (27.5)	—	—
JD	2 (5.00)	—	—
Samata	4 (10.0)	—	—
CPI	3 (7.5)	—	—
CPM	4 (10.00)	—	—
JMM	2 (5.0)	—	—
BPP	3 (7.50)	—	—
BSP	3 (7.5)	—	—
Total	**40 (100.00)**	**Total**	**40 (100.00)**

Eighteen respondents had joined a Political Party because they were attracted by the programmes of the Political Party. 3 were attracted by party leadership, 12 joined for social work and three said that they were forced by the Party (Table 43.3).

TABLE 43.3

Reasons for Membership

Reasons	N	%
Personal benefits	—	—
Suggested by elder	—	—
Forced by party	3	7.5
Attracted by party programme	18	45
Influenced by the personality of the leader in party	7	17.5
Social Work	12	30
Any other	—	—
Total	**40**	**100**

Participation in Party Activities

40 respondents had taken part in the activities of their party. 28 participated in processions, 18 in demonstrations, 13 had joined morchas, 15 had participated in political movements, 5 in satyagraha, and 5 in other activities (Table 44 and 44.1).

TABLE 44

Do You Participate in the Activities of Any Party?

Response	N	%
Yes	40	80
No	10	20
Total	**50**	**100**

TABLE 44.1

Activity

If yes, what activity?	N	%
Morcha	13	32.5
Procession	28	70
Demonstration	18	45
Satyagrah	5	12.5
Political Movement	15	37.5
Any other	5	12.5

Political Aspirations

35 respondents had some sort of political aspirations such as "to work for the party". Nine aspired to do social work, 3 wanted to work for the welfare of their caste, and five aspired for favour from their party leaders (Table 45 and 45.1).

TABLE 45

Do You have, Any Political Aspiration?

Response	N	%
Yes	35	70
No	15	30
Total	**50**	**100**

TABLE 45.1

If Yes, What

Political aspiration	N	%
Take to social work	9	25.71
Party work	18	51.43
Welfare of caste	3	8.57
Carrying favour or party leaders	5	14.28
Any other	—	—
Total	**35**	**100.00**

Voting

Voting is the most important political activity for majority of the citizens. All the respondents opined that voting is important in Democracy. Thirteen regarded it necessary because Democracy is the government for the people, of the people and by the people. 22 respondents believed that through Voting people could choose their representatives, 15 thought voting is necessary for the conduct of Indirect Democracy (Table 46).

49 respondents had voted in Lok Sabha General elections while just had voted first in Assembly elections (Table 47).

TABLE 46

Voting is Important for Democracy Why?

Response	*N*	%
Democracy is the Govt. of the people for the people, by the people	13	26
Voting indicates people choice of their representative	22	44
Voting is necessary in indirect Democracy	15	30
Any other	—	—
Total	**50**	**100**

TABLE 47

Have You Voted in Any Election?

Response	*N*	%
Lok Sabha	49	98
Assembly	1	2
Total	**50**	**100**

All the fifty respondents had voted in 1998 Lok Sabha Elections Five voted for Congress I because they were fascinated by the candidates personality, six voted for BJP because of the party image, 24 voted for JD because of the party's programme and manifesto, 11 voted for RJD due to caste consideration, 5 voted for Samata, 6 voted for Independents and 3 for BSP on other people's suggestion (Table 48 and 48.1).

TABLE 48

Were You a Voter in 1998 Lok Sabha Elections?

Response	*N*	%
Yes	50	100
No	—	—
Total	**50**	**100**

TABLE 48.1

If Yes, Name of the Party and Reason

Name of Party	*N(%)*	*Reason*	*N(%)*
Congress	5 (10%)	Fascinating personality	6 (12%)
BJP	6 (12%)	Party	18 (36%)
JD	24 (48%)	Party programme manifesto	22 (44%)
Janta Party RJD	11 (22%)	Caste	1 (2%)
Samata	5 (10%)	Religion	1 (2%)
Independent	6 (12%)	Suggested by other	1 (2%)
BSP	3 (6%)	Forced by other	1 (2%)
		Any other	—
Total	**50 (100%)**	**Total**	**50 (100%)**

The respondents were asked if they had voted in '95 Assembly elections in Bihar. All had voted. 14 had voted for JD due to party programes. 4 had voted for Congress I, 3 had voted for BJP. As regards reasons for voting, 20 had voted on party name, 26 (52%) had voted for party programme. Three (6%) had voted due to the charismatic personality of the candidate. One had voted on the suggestion of some other person, may be a relative, or a friend.

TABLE 49

Were You a Voter 1995 Assembly Election in Bihar?

Response	N	%
Yes	50	100
No	—	—
Total	**50**	**100**

TABLE 49.1

If Yes Name the Party and Reasons for Voting

Name of party	*N(%)*	*Reason*	*N(%)*
Congress	4 (8%)	Fascinating Personality	3 (6%)
BJP	3 (6%)	Party	20 (40%)
JD	14 (28%)	Party pogramme	26 (52%)
RJD	4 (8%)	Religion	—
Samata	1 (2%)	Suggested by other	1 (2%)
Independent	16 (32%)		
Shiv Sena	1 (2%)	—	
BSP	1 (2%)	—	
CPI ML	4 (8%)	—	
Socialist	1 (2%)	—	
Samajwadi	1 (2%)	—	
Total	**50 (100%)**	**Total**	**50 (100%)**

Canvassing

44 (88%) respondents had done canvassing for ther party candidates while only 6 (12%) had never taken part in this activity Out of the 24, the maximum number 20 had canvassed for Independent candidates. 11 (25%) had worked for RJD, seven for Janata Dal. Only 2 each had canvassed for Congress I and BJP, Regarding reasons, as many as 36 (81.82) had done it on party programme. Four (9.49) were influenced by the personality of the candidate. Two (4.54) had canvassed because the candidate was related to them, one on religious affinity, and on had done it just for 'Fun' (Table 50 and 50.1)

TABLE 50

Did You Take Part in Canvassing for Any Party in the Elections?

Response	N	%
Yes	44	88
No	6	12
Total	**50**	**100**

TABLE 50.1

Name of the Party and Reasons for Canvassing

Name of party	*N(%)*	*Reason*	*N(%)*
Congress	2 (4.54)	Party programme	36 (81.82)
BJP	2 (7.54)	Personality of the candidate	4 (9.09)
JD	7 (15.91)	Relation with the candidate	2 (4.54)
RJD	11 (25%)	Personal benefit	—
Independent	20 (45.45)	Religion	1 (2.27)
IPF	1 (2.7)	For fun	1 (2.27)
BPP	1 (2.27)	Any other	
Total	**44 (2.27)**	**Total**	**44 (100.00)**

Canvassing is an important activity in ensuring the electoral success of the contestants. Proper and wide canvassing help mobilization of the voters. Many start their political career as canvassers for any political party. A good canvasser becomes an asset for the party and gets closer to party leaders. When asked about canvassing, 44 (88%) respondents assured in the positive. They had taken part in canvassing. Although a good canvasser has qualities which are almost given by "nature", a lot depends also on how the canvassers are briefed by the party and candidate.

Decorum and dignity has to be cultivated in their behaviour, because the quality and level of the canvassers reflects the quality and level of the candidates personality.

Canvassing should be developed as an election strategy and people should be selected carefully by the candidate and party to do this job. Inclusion of ruffians and 'goonda elements' for canvassing may adversely affect the contestant and prejudice the voters against him/her.

The respondents were tested for their observation power regarding the election scenario. Ten (20%) noticed the operation of caste and communal interests during elections. Thirty-five (70%) pointed to "goonda elements" rampant during elections while 32 (64%) found group-interests and four observed extravagant use of money and one pointed to use of "muscle power". In all, the responses drew a negative and gloomy picture of election scene. May be, this could explain why women refrain from going to election booths for casting their votes. Similarly, these factors can also explain the hesitation of women in taking active part in electoral politics.

TABLE 51

Did You Notice the Following Elements Operating in the Elections?

Response	N	%
Castism and Communalism	10	20
Goondism	35	70
Groupism	32	64
Extravagance of money	4	8
Use of muscle power	1	2
Any other	—	—

The responses point to the urgent need of developing norms and measures for the conduct of voting in a peaceful and civilized manner. Severe restrictive measures need to be implemented to check 'goonda elements' operating during elections. The Election Commission has laid out various norms, but it needs the support of the general voters, bureaucracy and above all the politicians who are the root of such disturbances.

Contesting Elections is an Urgent Need of Political Participation

32 (64%) respondents did express their desire to contest elections. Among them 22 wanted to contest elections because they desired to serve people. 8 wanted to contest for social prestige while 2 expressed power as the main reason behind their desire for contesting elections. Among those who did not want to contest elections three gave lack of funds as the reason. Four blamed the political parties for their apathy in giving ticket to women while eleven respondents did not want to partake in elections because of increasing violence during elections (Table 52 and 52.1).

TABLE 52

Do You Desire to Contest Elections?

Response	*N*	*%*
Yes	32	64
No	18	36
Total	**50**	**100**

TABLE 52.1

If Yes	*N (%)*	*If No*	*N (%)*
Desire to serve people	22 (68.75)	Lack of funds	3 (16.67)
For Power	2 (6.25)	Apathy of Political Parties in giving ticket to women	4 (22.22)
For Social Prestige	8 (25%)	Increasing Violence During election	11 (61.11)
		Any other	—
Total	**32 (100.00)**	**Total**	**18 (100.00)**

When asked how many times they had contested Lok Sabha and/or Vidhan Sabha elections, the response showed that 46 had contested Assembly elections out of which 26 had fought on party ticket while 20 had contested elections as independent candidates. Two had contested Lok Sabha elections as Independent while 2 had contested Lok Sabha elections on party ticket. Among these 22 contestants who had fought elections independently 14 had never associated themselves with any party ever. The other had been in some political party or other, but fought election independently because they did not get party ticket. For example Anju Devi was in Janata Dal but did not get ticket, so she fought election as an Independent candidate. She is now in RJD Kiran Sinha fought election as Independent when she did not get ticket, from Janata Dal. In all seven contested independently who were earlier members of Janata Dal but did not get party ticket. Three were members of Janata Party but had to contest as Independent because they did not get party ticket. Two fought as Independents because they did not get ticket from their party-Congress I (Table 53, 53.1 and 53.2).

TABLE 53

How Many of You have Contested Elections Independently and/or as Party Candidate?

	Lok Sabha N(%)	*Assembly* N(%)	*Total*
Party Candidate	2 (17.14)	26 (92.86)	28
As Independent	2 (9.09)	20 (90.90)	22
Total	**4 (8%)**	**46 (92%)**	**50**

TABLE 53.1

Those Who Fought Elections as Independent Candidates, Did You Ever Associate with Any Party?

Party	*N*	%
Always as Independent Candidate	14	63.64
Have been in Political Party but contested as Independent	8	36.36
Total	**22**	**100.00**

TABLE 53.II

Those Who Fought on Party Ticket, Name Your Party

Name of Party	N	%
Congress	2	7.14
BJP	1	3.57
JD	7	25.00
CPM	2	7.14
RJD	1	3.57
CPI ML	4	14.28
CPI	2	7.14
Others	9	32.14
Total	**28**	**100.00**

The response amplify that some sort of support system needs to be developed by the State to fund women who are contesting as Independent candidates. Parties should be compelled to put up more women candidates. As the records show the percentage of electoral success of women in relation to their candidature is much higher than male candidates.

A word of caution for women contestants—they should contest elections only after developing their area base or 'Constituency' and work seriously in public life, before rushing to fight elections

Change in party membership has become a common feature of present political situation.

Among the total respondents 32, (64%) had changed party membership. Only 18 had always struck to their party in all situations.

Regarding reasons for changing party membership. 7 had done it due to change in party ideology, while 18 had changed because of rift in the party. Four had changed party due to party's electoral failure. 2 did it because they felt that their party was loosing its esteem while one respondent changed her party in the desire to win election (Table 54 and 54.1)

TABLE 54

Have You Ever Changed Party Membership

	N	%
Yes	32	64
No	18	36
Total	**50**	**100**

TABLE 54.1

Reasons for Changing Party Membership

Response	*N*	%
Change in party ideology	7	21.87
Rift in Party	18	56.25
Failure of the party in election	4	12.5
Desire to win in elections	1	3.12
Low esteem of the party	2	6.25
Total	**32**	**100.00**

The respondents were asked to give their opinion on anti-defection law, 28 expressed their approval while 22 disagreed (Table 55)

TABLE 55

Do You Approve of Anti-defection Law?

Response	*N*	%
Yes	28	56
No	22	44
Total	**50**	**100**

Regarding reason 14 out of 28 approve because it will check corruption in Politics. Seven support it because it will bring stability to government. Seven support it because it will increase. Party discipline. Among those who disapprove of Anti-defection law, 11 think it will check the arbitrariness of party leadership, 6 believe that secondary level leaders will get a change to reach top positions while 5 believe that small parties will get a chance in politics (Table 55.1).

TABLE 55.1

If Approve-If Disapprove

Reasons	*N (%)*	*Reasons*	*N (%)*
It will check corruption in Politics	14 (50%)	Party leadership will not be arbitrary	11 (50%)
It will bring stability to Government	7 (25%)	Secondary level Leaders will get a chance to reach top position	6
It will increase party Discipline	7 (25%)	Small Parties will get a chance in Politics	5
Total	**28 (100%)**	**Total**	**22 (100%)**

Forty-six respondents believe that party support is necessary for contesting elections. Eleven think that it provides a platform to the contestant to express his/her views to the voters, 8 opine that party gives strength two think it helps to influence the voter favourably while nine hit the very crucial factor—it helps with funds (Table 56).

TABLE 56

Do You Believe that Party Support is Necessary for Contesting Election?

If Yes, why?	N	*If No*
Party provides a Platform	16 (34.78)	4 (100.00)
Gives Publicity	11 (23.91)	
Party strength	8 (17.39)	
Influences the electorate in favour	2 (4.34)	
Provides funds	9 (19.56)	
Any other		
Total	46 (100.00)	4 (100.00)

Regarding the issue of 33% reservation for women in Lok Sabha and State Assemblies—47 were in favour. As regards reasons for their opinion 20 respondents agreed that when women are in increased number they will be able to place the problems of women in the Lok Sabha and will be able to emphasize the implementation of remedial measures. 10 respondents opined that political parties will be forced to give ticket to women 12 thought that women will be provided with more opportunities to participate in elections. Four respondents were of the opinion that the presence of women will be felt in Lok Sabha and Vidhan Sabha. Three respondents did not favour reservation. One opined that reservation was against the principles of Democracy, while one thought that it will only benefit the elite class, and one thought that problems of the common women will not be highlighted (Table 57).

TABLE 57

What is Your Reaction Towards 33% Reservation for Women?

If Yes	*N (%)*	*If No*	*N (%)*
It will make easy for Women to fight election	12 (25.53)	It is against the Principle of Democracy	1 (33.33)
Parties will be forced to put up women candidate	11 (21.27)	Only elite women will benefit	1 (33.33)
Their presence in the Lok Sabha and Vidhan Sabha will be felt	4 (8.51)	Problem of the common women will not be highlighted	1 (33.33)
They will bring up problems of women in these Sabhas and force remedies	20 (42.55)	It will affect smooth working of the Sabha	—
For to be taken up	1 (2.12)	Because most of the women will be inexperienced	—
—	—	Any other	—
Total	**47 (100.00)**	**Total**	**3 (100.00)**

The responses amplify that women contestants loose heavily

in elections because they are not given enough importance by their parties, and they have to fight election as independent candidates without the support of any party. As the response clarifies, 28 out of 50 respondents fought elections as Independent candidates.

The contestants have frequently changed their parties. In this sample, the maximum number of women who contested as Independents had been associated with Janta Dal. They left their party during '95 elections and later joined BJP or RJD when there was a split in Janta Dal.

Among those who fought on party ticket, the contestants from Left parties suffered badly. A contestant like Saroj Chaube of CPI ML has never won election, although she is a hardcore activists, a powerful orator and organizer. Lack of funds may be supposed to be one reason. Another reason may be that CPI ML has not been able to get a hold over the Urban voters. Another CPI ML candidate is Dr. Shahida Hasan, a Medical Doctor by profession, very dedicated having clear conception and a hard. core activists. She lost '95 assembly elections. In all 4 CPI ML candidates, 2 from CPM and 2 from CPI lost elections. The maximum number of defeated candidates are from Janta Dal, seven.

7

Women in Political Decision-making (MLA's, MP's and Ministers)

Decision-making bodies are at the apex of total Political structure. In a democratic polity it is required and expected that all segments of a country's population based on religion, costs (in the case of India), languages, race, ethnicity and more importantly Gender as a segments which cuts across all other segments and formulates the largest single group of the population, is ensured adequate presence and participation, so that the public policies thus formulated reflect the demands and interests of all diverse groups. Unfortunately the largest group of women has a almost scarce presence in the decision-making bodies such as the Legislative and the Executive. The presence of women reflects just a 'token' of a gender representation in such bodies. The All India tally is very low, and Bihar cannot be expected to go a very different way.

Bihar

The total number of women from Bihar in the thirteen Lok Sabha's (1952-1999) is Fifty. Of course we have to remember that Bihar till recently has had 54 seats in Lok Sabha. After the creation of Jharkhand it now has 36 seats. The average percentage of women MP's from Bihar is not difficult to guess. The average in the Rajya Sabha is no letter. In the Bihar Vidhan Sabha the total number of women legislators for all the thirteen Vidhan Sabha's is 183. The number of persons is actually less because many have repeated their success three to four times.

Therefore the 4th category of our respondents consists of members of the Lok Sabha, Rajya Sabha and Union Cabinet from Bihar and members of the Bihar Vidhan Sabha, Vidhan Parishad and Council of Ministers of the State. In all, fifty respondents were selected from this special category. Efforts was made to cover almost the five decades, since Independence, all the regions in the State, Castes, religion, different cultural shades etc. Among the 50 respondents we have taken thirteen Ministers, nine MP's and 24 MLA's in proportion to the number of women who have been are ministers, legislators and members of the Parliament. This chapter contains analysis of the responses of such respondent, regarding their socio-economic cultural background, their perception of the self (as women), their political aptitudes and awareness of Politics—forms of governance, political institutions, political ideologies, leaders etc, and finally their career history and also their participation as Voters, canvassers and their opinion on current and controversial socio-political issues such as 33% reservation for women, creation of Jharkhand State (the data was collected during '98 and early '99) Anti-defection law etc.

This category contains women who are "political elites". The composition and character of the "Political Elite" has been changing constantly over the decades. The socio-economic and educational background of this category has also been changing. Levels of education of the earlier women legislators was definitely of a much higher level as the responses and case histories have revealed. The caste composition especially in the context of Bihar has changed. We are witnessing the entry of Backward Caste women in reasonable number. The hold of and majority presence of upper caste women is still there, but space has been created also for semi-literate backward caste women. The Rashtriya Janata Dal has been putting up women candidates and they are winning too due to the support of the party.

As the socio-economic and educational background of Individuals patently affects their behaviour and various activities in adult life, it necessary to know about the background of the respondents, to understand and evaluate their political aptitude, awareness and more importantly, their level of political participation.

Socio-economic and Cultural Backgrounds

Social. The social factors identified are religion, caste and sub-caste, age, place of birth and residence, type of family, marriage details etc.

Religion. 98% of the respondents are Hindu and only 2% are Christian. The Hindu respondents have been further categorized according to caste in the categories of Upper Castes, Backward Castes, Scheduled Castes and Scheduled Tribes.

Upper Castes. The highest number (10) come from Bhumihar caste, followed by Rajputs (7) and Kayastha (3) and Brahmins (4). The total number of upper caste respondents is 24. Thus about 48.5% Hindu respondents come from upper caste.

Backward Castes. The total of such respondents is 20 (40.5) out of which the Yadav take the narrow lead (6) followed by Baniyas (5) other Backward Castes (5) and Kurmis (4).

Scheduled Castes. Just two respondents are from the caste of Dusadh.

Scheduled Tribes. Four respondents are from Santhal tribes.

In all 48.5% of the respondents belong to upper castes, 40% are from Backward Castes, 4% from Scheduled Castes and 4.5% from Scheduled Tribes (Tables 1 and 2).

TABLE 1

Religion of Respondent

Religion	*N*	%
Hindu	49	98.00
Muslim	—	—
Sikh	—	—
Christian	1	2.00
Total	**50**	**100.00**

TABLE 2

Caste and Sub-Caste of Respondent

Upper Caste	*N(%)*	*Backward Caste*	*N(%)*	*Scheduled Caste*	*N(%)*	*Scheduled Tribe*	*N(%)*
Brahmin	4 (16.67)	Yadav	6 (30)	Musahar	—	Santhal	3 (100)
Rajput	7 (28.16)	Kurmi	4 (20)	Dusadh	2 (100)	Bhil	—
Bhumihar	10 (41.67)	Baniya	5 (25)	Chamar	—	Other	—
Kayastha	3 (12)	Other	5 (25)	Other	—	—	—
Total	**24 (48.97)**	**Total**	**20 (40.81)**	**Total**	**2 (4.08)**	**Total**	**3 (6.12)**

(Figure in bracket means percentage)

Age of Respondents

About 27 respondents (54%) belong to the age-group of 50 and above, while 17 (34%) are from 35-40 age group. Only 3 (6%) are in the age group of 25-35 years and similarly 3 (6%) are from the younger age group of 18 to 25 years (Table 3).

TABLE 3

Age of Respondent

Age group	*N*	*%*
18-25	3	6.00
25-35	3	6.00
35-50	17	34.00
50 and above	27	54.00
Total	**50**	**100.00**

Place of Birth

64 (32%) of the respondents were born in village, 16 (32%) in town, and just 2 (4%) in city. 8% of the respondents have spent their early life in villages and just one is living at present in village. 88% of the respondents (44) lived mostly in villages in

their early life, 30 (60%) are at present living in towns. 19 are at present living in city.

The Table reflects that majority of the respondents were born in village and spent most of their early life in towns. Majority of living in towns at present and only 19 are living in cities at present. The reflection is that the majority of respondents have a rural and sub-urban background (Table 4).

TABLE 4

Place of Birth and Early Life Spent

Place	*Place of birth*	*Live most early life*	*Live at present*
Village	32 (64%)	4 (8%)	1 (2%)
Town	16(32%)	44 (88%)	30 (60%)
City	2 (4%)	2(4%)	19(38%)
Total	**50(100%)**	**50(100%)**	**50(100%)**

Marriage

45 out of the 50 respondents are presently married which constitutes 90% of the respondents. There is one case of a divorcee while 4 are widows.

TABLE 5

Marital Status of Respondent

Marital Status	*N*	*%*
Married	45	90
Unmarried	—	—
Divorced	1	2
Widowed	4	8
Total	**50**	**100**

Table shows that 49 respondents were married comparatively early, in the 15-25 age group. Only one respondent married late (Table 5 and 6).

The pattern of marriage of respondents emphasizes early

marriage and the very traditional social character of Bihari women. Their coming into politics is very much in consonance with social culture, custom and tradition in Bihar.

TABLE 6

Age of Marriage of Respondent

Age of marriage	N	%
15-25	49	98
25 and above	1	2
Total	**50**	**100**

Family Pattern

Nearly 56% (23) of respondents belong to Joint Family structure. 38% (1) live in Extended Families and only 16% (8) belong to Nuclear Family pattern (Table 7).

TABLE 7

Type of Family of Respondent

Type	N	%
Nuclear	8	16
Extended	19	38
Joint	23	56
Total	**50**	**100**

The Family background of the respondents affirms that the respondents belong to a very traditional family structure. Joint Family System signifies agricultural and/or business economic background and in a way is very helpful for women in Politics because it gives them freedom to a certain extent from household responsibilities, and they can devote more time outside. Further, strength of the family behind them helps build up their social image, interpersonal contact and communication and workforce at the time of election campaigns.

Education

The total respondents are educated with varying degree of academic levels. About 25 (50%) of the respondents are graduates,

12 (24%) are educated upto Secondary level. Three respondents have Masters degree, 4 have post-graduate (Ph.D.) degrees. Three have law degree while 3 have B.Ed degree, out of the total of 50, 40 have general education degree while ten have technical/ professional degree. None have a Medical or Engineering degree or Management/ Computer education degree (Table 8 and 8.1).

TABLE 8

Educational Status of Respondent

Educational Status	*N*	*%*
Educated	50	100
Uneducated	—	—
Total	**50**	**100.00**

TABLE 8.1

Educational Level

Educational Level	*N(%)*	*Technical Education*	*N(%)*
Primary	—	B.Ed.	3 (30.00)
Secondary	12 (30.00)	Ph.D.	4 (40.00)
Graduate	25 (62.5)	LL.B.	3 (30.00)
P.G.	3 (7.5)	Engg.	—
–	–	Management	—
Total	**40 (100.00)**	**Total**	**10 (100.0)**

Occupation

All the Fifty respondents are working. 44 out of 50 are engaged in politics and social work. Five are in regular service while 1 is engaged in business (Table 9 and 9.1)

TABLE 9

Occupation of Respondent

Marital Status	*N*	%
Housewife	—	
Working	50	100
Total	**50**	**100**

TABLE 9.1

Occupation

Occupation	*N*	%
Politics+Social work	44	88
Service	5	10
Business	1	2
Total	**50**	**100**

Monthly Income

Thirty-eight (76%) respondents are earning Rupees Ten Thousand and or above per month. Nine have a monthly income ranging between Rupees 5000 to 10.000. Three respondents are in the monthly income group of Rupees 2000-5000 per month.

In all 76% are in the middle to upper middle income group. Only 3 belong to low income group (Table 10).

TABLE 10

Monthly Income of Respondent

Income	*N*	%
1000-2000	—	
2000-3000	3	6
5000-10000	9	18
10000- above	38	76
Total	**50**	**100**

Perception of the Self (Women)

It is a known fact that achievement of an individual is guided very much by his/her perception of the self. If a person has a low image of the self, he or she will not be able to go ahead which ever field it may be. As for 'Polities', it is basically a "achievement quest" activity. It deals with "power" and 'influence' and to acquire these qualities it is necessary to have a very positive image of self. Besides perception of the self as an individual, it is also required that one has a high image of the 'category', section, group one belongs to. Women have been marginalized to politics for centuries. Why is it so? Thus it have anything to do with low image or perception negative of the self as 'woman'? Has she been socialized to believe that women by nature are not inclined towards achievement, and search for power?

To find answers to such issues, respondents were asked a few questions about their perception of the self?

Q.1. Do you think women enjoy and equal status with males in real life? 37 (74%) respondents believe that women do not enjoy equal status with men in real life. Only 13 believe that they do. This reflects that women regard men as very superior to women, and therefore their status is unequal (Table 11).

TABLE 11

Do You Think that Women Enjoy an Equal Status with Men in Real Life

Response	*N*	%
Yes	13	26
No	37	74
Total	**50**	**100**

Q.2. (a) Do believe that men are superior to women by nature?

Thirteen responded to this question out of which nine opined that society gives men more prominent position than women. Three believed that men were physically stronger than women.

TABLE 12.1

Do You Believe that Men are Superior to Women?

If Yes	N	%
They are physically stronger than women	1	7.69
Socket gives them permanent place	9	69.2
Usually they earn better	3	23.7
Total	**13**	**100.0**

Q.2. (b) 37 respondents disagreed with Q. 2(a) and 20 opined that women were important because they brought up the next generation in right direction. 17 opined that women played an equally important role and performed duties as men in society Table 12-1 and 12-2.

TABLE 12. 2

If No	N	%
Women perform an important duty in society as men	17	45.9
Women are important for bringing up the next generation in right direction	20	54.0
Total	**37**	**100.0**

TABLE 13

Should Women be Educated? Yes or No?

Response *If yes, women be educated till which level*	N	%
Primary	—	
Secondary	3	6
Graduate	37	74
Post Graduate	4	8
Technical degree	6	12
No, women be no educated	—	
Total	50	100

Role of Education

The respondents were asked whether women should be educated. This question was asked keeping in mind the role education plays in enhancing the image of the self. 37 (74%) respondents were in favour of Graduate level education for women. Only 4 respondents preferred Post-graduate level and 6 were in favour of Technical Education (Table 13).

The next question linked to this issue was whether the status of educated women is superior to uneducated women. 48 respondents believed that educated women enjoyed a better status. Only 2 respondents thought that education did not make any difference in the status of women (Table 14).

TABLE 14

Do You Think that the Status of Educated Women is Superior to Uneducated Women?

Status of educated	N	%
Superior	48	96
Inferior	—	
Equal	2	4
No Opinion	—	
Total	**50**	**100**

Full-Time Career

The respondents were asked to give their opinion regarding the importance of full-time career for the status of women. 42 responded in favour. Twenty-two among the respondents believed that it gives confidence to the women. The reason 14 gave was that it gives economic independence and 6 believed that it enhances the social status of women.

Eight respondents were against full-time career for women. The reasons put forward were:

It leads to family break up	4 respondents
Temperament and physical frailty makes the job tough	3 respondents
Any other	

(Table 15.1 and 15.2)

TABLE 15.1

Do vou Believe in Full Time Career for Women?

If Yes, why?	*N*	%
It gives confidence	22	52.38
It gives economic independence	14	33.33
It gives better status in society	6	14.28
Total	**42**	**100.00**

Table 15.2

If No, why?	*N*	%
Economic Independence may break the family	4	50
Temperament and physical ability may make the job tough	3	37.5
Any other	1	12.5
Total	**8**	**100.0**

The responses reflect that the respondents do not have a very positive perception of the self as women. Thirty-seven out of 50 believed that women have a status unequal to men. As regards natural superiority of men and luckily very few responded were in favour only thirteen. Some did hit the truth by maintaining that society gave them superior status and also because they earned and earned better. About 37 (74%) did not consider men to be superior and did try to reiterate the important roles played by women.

As regards the role of education and full-time career in enhancing and making perception of the self more positive in women, the responses were very positive. However, the maximum number supported Graduate level education for women, which reflected that they were not in tune with the existing situation in linking up education with career. Not many supported technical education which is at present the sought after requirement for jobs.

Political Aptitude and Awareness

The third part of schedule consisted of questions responses to which would clarify the political aptitude and awareness of respondents.

Political Aptitude

Two questions were put to the respondents to gauze their political aptitude which are as follows:

1. Would you approve of political career for women?

   Part (B) of A asked their opinion on reasons listed for their approval and disapproval.

2. Would women be successful in Political leadership positions?

   37 respondents have strongly approved of political career for women while 13 approve. Thus it seems all the respondents have very positive opinion about political career for women. They have come into politics because they have this positive aptitude. Coming to reasons for their approval, about 54% (27) think that a political career will improve the life conditions of women and 23 opine that the presence of women in politics will clean politics (Table 16 and 16.1).

TABLE 16

Would You Approve of Political Career for Women?

Response	*N*	%
Strongly approve	37	74
Approve	13	26
Strongly disapprove	—	
Disapprove	—	
No Opinion	—	
Total	**50**	**100**

TABLE 16.1

Approve and Disapprove

If approve	*N(%)*	*If disapprove*	*N(%)*
(i) Entering politics will improve life condition	27 (54%)	It creates tension in family	—
(ii) Women entrance may cleanse politics	23 (46%)	Damage their image	—
		Lack of temperament and physical ability makes the job tough	—
		It involves a lot of money, increasing use of muscle power	
Total	**50 (100%)**		

In response to the second question 26 respondents (52%) believe that women could be successful political leaders because they are on equal footing with men. 14 opine that the constitution guarantees equal political rights and ten believe that their achievements and presence in politics ensure successful leadership for them (Table 17).

TABLE 17

Would Women be Successful in Political Leadership Position?

If yes, Reason	*N(%)*	*If no, Reason*	*N(%)*
She is on equal footing with men in this regard	26 (52%)	Lack of social interaction	—
Our constitution guarantees equal political right	14 (28%)	Lack of hard work and toughness	—
Her achievement in political field itself in her qualification to success	10 (20%)	Damaging to image and character	—
		Criminalisation of politics	-
Total	50 (100.0)	Total	—

Political Awareness

A set of questions were put to the respondents to verify their awareness of the political structures, leaders etc.

TABLE 18

Given Below are Names of Five Important Women, Who Among them are Politically Important?

	N	%
(i) Mother Teressa	—	
(ii) Begum Khalida Zia	48	96
(iii) Indira Gandhi	50	100
(iv) Margaret Thatcher	46	92
(v) Medha Patekar	50	100

In the first question a set of names of five important women was put to them to identify those who were known political leaders. All the respondents identified Indira Gandhi and Margaret Thatcher as important political personalities. They could also identify Begum Khalida Zia and socio-political activist Medha Patkar (Table 18).

TABLE 19

Did Indira Gandhi as Prime Minister Raise the Over all Status of Indian Women?

If Yes	*N*	%
1. She became a role model	17	34
2. Defied the myth that "women are no good in politics"	7	14
3. Social attitude towards women changed	6	12
4. No, Indira Gandhi the overall status of women did not change	20	40
Total	50	100

In the next question respondents were asked to respond whether Indira Gandhi as Prime Minister helped raise the overall status of women. 17 respondents believed that she became a role model for women, 7 believed that her success defied the myth that "women are no good in politics", 6 respondents believed that her success changed social attitude towards women, but 20 respondents opined that the success of Indira Gandhi as Prime Minister did not make any substantial difference in the status of common women (Table 19).

Regarding questions related to the political pattern of governance in India several questions were asked

(a) The present pattern of Indian Government;

(b) Which form of government is more suitable for India

(c) Names of five important Political Parties at national level.

(d) Five important Political Parties of regional level including Bihar.

In response to (a) 47 respondents identified the present Indian Government as Parliamentary form of Government. All the respondents favoured Democracy as the most suitable form of Government for India (Table 20 and 21).

TABLE 20

What Pattern of Government Does India have at Present?

Pattern	N	%
Parliamentary	47	94.0
Presidential	—	
Unitary	—	
Federal	3	6.0
Total	**50**	**100.0**

TABLE 21

Which Form of Govt. Do You Consider to be More Suitable for India?

Form of Govt.	N	%
Democracy	50	100.0
Aristocracy	—	
Dictatorship	—	
Total	**50**	**100.0**

In (c) the responses graded Congress I and BJP on the first position. Janata Dal was placed on a second rank while CPI and CPM were placed third. (Table 22).

TABLE 22

Name Five Important Political Parties of National Level

Name of Parties	N	%
B.J.P.	50	100
Congress	50	100
J.D.	46	92
C.P.I.	43	86
C.P.M.	38	76

Regarding regional level parties (with reference to Bihar) Rashtriya Janta Dal got the maximum support with 42 respondents (Table 23).

TABLE 23

Name Five Important Political Parties of Regional Level Including Bihar

Name political parties regional	N	%
B.J.P.	50	100
R.J.D.	42	84
J.M.M.	35	70
Akali Dal	38	76
AIDMK	33	66
Shiv Sena	31	62

To cross-check their awareness about Political parties the respondents were given a set of names of Political Parties and were asked to identify national level parties. All the respondents identified BJP and Congress I Janata Dal was identified by 46, CPI ML by 43 and CPM by 38 respondents. Only 12 identified Samata Party (Table 24).

TABLE 24

Given Below are the Names of Political Parties Tick Mark National Level Parties

Name of Parties	N	%
R.J.D.	—	
J.M.M.	2	4
B.S.P.	—	
B.J.P.	50	100
Samata Party	12	24
CPI ML	43	86
Janata Dal	46	92
D.M.K.	—	
Congress	50	100
C.P.M.	38	76
Forward Bloc	—	
J.M.M.	—	

To cross-check the awareness of the respondents about political leaders, a set of names of important personalities was given to them. All respondents identified Mahatma Gandhi, Jawahar Lal Nehru and Jai Prakash Narain. Lal Bahadur Shastri and Mao-Tse-Tung were identified simultaneously by 48 and 42 respondents. Only 13 could identify Karl Marx (Table 25).

TABLE 25

Given Below are the Names Often Important Persons of the World Which of Them Were Political Leaders?

Response	N	%
Martin Luther King	—	
Mother Teressa	—	
Mahatma Gandhi	50	100
Karl Marx	13	26
Swami Vivekanand	—	
Jai Prakash Narain	50	100
Jawahar Lal Nehru	50	100
Mao-Tse-Tung	42	96
Rabindra Nath Tagore	—	
Lal Bahadur Shastri	48	96
Pt. Ravi Shankar	—	

The respondents were asked to name five important women in Indian Politics, Indira Gandhi and Sarojini Naidu were named by all the respondents. The other names mentioned were Tarkeshwari Sinha by 48, Sucheta Kripalani by 46 and Nazma Heptullah by 44.

TABLE 26

Name Five Important Women in Indian Politics

Name	N	%
Indira Gandhi	50	100
Sarojini Naidu	50	100
Sucheta Kripalani	46	92
Tarkeshwari Sinha	48	96
Nazma Heptullah	44	88

A set of names of different fields was given to the respondents to identify political leaders from the set Indira Gandhi and Sarojini Naidu were identified as Political leaders by all the respondents. A surprising recognition by all was of the famous environmentalists Medha Patkar as an important political leaders (Table 26 and 27).

TABLE 27

Below are Names of Some Important Women in India Who Among Them is a Political Leader?

Response	N	%
Mahadevi Verma	—	
Medha Patekar	5C	100
M.S. Subhlaxmi	—	
Indira Gandhi	50	100
Sarojini Naidu	50	100

Bihar. The respondents were asked to name five important women in Bihar Politics. Krishna Shahi was named by all while Tarkeshwari Sinha was named by 48, Prabhawati Gupta by 47 Ram Dulari Sinha by 46 and Uma Pandey by 44 respondents (Table 28).

TABLE 28

Name Five Important Women in Politics in Bihar

Name of women	N	%
Tarkeshwari Sinha	48	96
Uma Pandey	44	88
Ram Dulari Sinha	46	92
Krishna Shahi	50	100
Prabhawati Gupta	47	94

The respondents were asked to name five important political leaders of Bihar. Dr. Rajendra Prasad was named by all while Jagjivan Ram was named by 48, Karpoori Thakur by 44, Laloo Prasad Yadav by 43 and Kedar Pandey by 42 respondents (Table 29).

TABLE 29

Name Five Important Political Leaders in Bihar

Name of political leader	N	%
Dr. Rajendra Prasad	50	100
Kedar Pandey	42	84
Laloo Prasad Yadav	43	86
Jagjiwan Ram	48	96
Karpoori Thakur	44	88

The respondents were asked to name the Ruling Party in Bihar and the total response was Rashtriya Janta Dal while Bharatiya Janta Party was named as the main opposition party by all the respondents (Table 30 and 31).

TABLE 30

Which Party is Ruling in Bihar at Present (1998-99) and Which as the Opposition Party in Bihar Legislative Assembly

Ruling party	N	*Opposition party*	N
R.J.D.	50 (100%)	B.J.P.	50 (100%)

The respondents were asked to opine if the ruling government would be able to complete its five year term. 32 respondents were positive while 18 were in doubt. As we all know, the government did complete its term and new elections were held in year 2000 (Table 31).

TABLE 31

Do You Think that the Present Govt. (1998-99) Will Complete its Five Year Term?

Response	*N*	%
Yes	32	64
No	18	36
Total	**50**	**100**

The respondents were asked whether they were in favour of a separate Jharkhand State. 31 respondents were in favour while 19 were against it. The data was collected between late '98 and early '99. The Jharkhand State did come into existence on 15.11.2000 (Table 32).

TABLE 32

Are You in Favour of Separate Jharkhand State

Response	*N*	%
Yes	31	62
No	19	38
N.R.	—	
Total	**50**	**100**

Caste. Plays a very crucial role in the conduct of 'Polities' in Bihar. Therefore the respondents were asked to state whether caste was the 'bane' of Politics in Bihar. 43 respondents did believe that it was, while, 7 did not agree to this.

Regarding reasons, among those 43 who agreed that caste was the bane of politics in Bihar, 19 agreed that voting on caste-lines prohibits the entry of able persons in Politics, while 14 believed that caste considerations would obstruct the Government working for the welfare of all people. Ten respondents agreed to the reason that it leads to social tensions (Table 33 and 33.1).

TABLE 33

Caste is the Bane of Politics in Bihar—Do You Agree?

Response	N	%
Yes	43	86
No	7	14
Total	**50**	**100**

TABLE 33.1

	N(%)		N(%)
(i) Voting on caste basis prohibits, able persons to come in politics	19 (44%)	It will demolish upper caste hegemony in Bihar politics	2 (28.57)
(ii) It leads to social tensions	10 (23.25)	The backward and lower caste will get a chance to enter politics	5 (31.43)
iii) The Govt. does not work for the welfare of all people	14 (32.56)	It will bring social Justice	—
Total	**43 (100.0)**	**Total (100.0)**	**7 100.00**

The respondents were asked to evaluate the Government in Bihar by giving their opinion as regards the level of corruption. 43 respondents agreed that the Government was totally corrupt and among them 28 agreed to the reason that law and order maintaining institutions are totally corrupt in Bihar, and no one is safe. 16 blamed the importance given to caste as the main reason of corruption (Table 34).

TABLE 34

Do You Agree that Politics in Bihar is Totally Corrupt?

If Yes, give reason	*N(%)*	*If No, give reason*	*N(%)*
1. Caste-based	6 (13.95)	Expediency is the rule in Politics	4 (57.14)

(Contd.)

(Contd. Table 34)

2. Corruption in Politics	9 (20.93)	There is no Caste corruption	2 (28.57)
3. Law and order is non-existent in Bihar	28 (65.11)	Partial corruption is every where	1 (14.28)
Total	**43 (100.0)**	**Total**	**7 (100.0)**

TABLE 35

In Your Opinion What is the Mark of Good Govt.?

Response	*N*	%
Stability	18	36
Free of corruption	13	26
Concern for the welfare of all the citizen	16	32
Any other	3	6
Total	**50**	**100**

The respondents were asked to identify the mark of a good government. 'Stability' was given by 18 respondents as the mark of good government. 16 respondents favoured concern for the welfare of all as an important mark, whereas thirteen opined that a good government should be free of corruption (Table 35).

Participation in Politics

Part IV of the schedule consists of questions designed to trace the participation of respondents in Politics—the various levels at which they participated, the influences that shaped their political career, their age of entry into politics, their knowledge of political literature.

TABLE 36

Participation in Politics

Active in Politics	*N*	%	*Age of joining Politics*	*N*	%
Yes	50	100	20-35	49	98
No -			35-50	1	2
Total	**50**	**100**	**Total.**	**50**	**100**

Obviously all the respondents in this category are active or have been active in Politics. 49 (98%) respondents record that they joined politics in the age group of 20-35 years. Only one respondent joined in the age-group of 35-50 years. A late entry, so to say (Table 36).

It has been a persistent observation especially in Bihar that male relatives, mostly husband and/ or Fathers have influenced women's entry into Politics. The responses confirm this notion. 27 (54%) respondents accept that their fathers had a lot of influence in this decision while 14 (28%) have regarded their husbands influence as important. Four respondents were influenced by their mothers and incidentally two of them had mothers in Politics. Four respondents were influenced by speeches of some leaders while one was influenced by a friend (Table 37).

TABLE 37

Who Influenced Your Entry into Politics? Is Any Family Member in Politics

Active in Politics	N	%	*Age of joining Politics*	N	%
Father	27	54	Father	12	24
Mother	4	8	Mother	2	4
Brother	—		Brother	1	2
Sister			Sister	—	
Friend	1	2	Husband	24	48
Husband	14	28	In-law	6	12
In-laws			No body in Politics	5	10
Books					
Speech of leader	4	8			
Total	50	100.0	**Total**	50	100.0

Many of the respondents have had either father or mother or husband active in politics. Husbands of 24 (48%) respondents are or have been in politics while fathers of 12 respondents have been in politics. Two respondents have had mothers active in politics. Only 5 respondents have not had any relative actively engaged in Politics.

Reading Political Literature

The respondents were asked whether they liked to read or had read political literature. Forty-four (88%) respondents had read and liked to read literature on Democracy, while 3 respondents were well-versed in literature on communism. 47 respondents liked to be in touch with political literature (Table 38 and 38.1).

TABLE 38

Do You Read Political Literature

Type of literature	*Yes (N)*	*No (N)*
On democracy	44	88
On communism	3	6
On dictatorship		
Any other	3	6
Total	**50**	**100**

TABLE 38.1

If yes, give reason	*N(%)*	*If no, give reason*	*N(%)*
Liking	47 (94%)	Not permitted by elder	—
Getting free of charge	1 (2%)	No liking	—
Compelled by party	—	Short of time	—
Forced by elders	—	Any other	—
Any other	2 (4%)		
Total	**50 (100.0)**		

42 (87.5) attended such meetings for subjects discussed. 28 attended to understand party politics, 38 attended because issues of national and international affairs interested them. 27 (56.2) attended study circles organized to discuss Democracy related issues (Table 39 and 39.1).

TABLE 39

Do You Attend Political Meetings

If yes, on what	N(%)	No, do not attend political meeting
Oratory of the Speaker	3 (2.25)	2(100.0)
His/Her personality	3 (6.25)	—
His/Her views	4 (8.33)	
Programme of the party	38(79.17)	
\ny other		
Total	**48(100.0)**	**2(100.0)**

TABLE 39.1

Do You Attend Study Circles Organized by Any Political Party?

Total	**43**	**Total**	**7**
If yes, give details	N	*If no, give details*	N
Subject discussed	42 (87.5)	Elder do not allowing	—
Party politics	28 (58.34)	No liking	2 (100.0)
National and International Affairs	38 (79.17)	Waste of time	—
Policies of other parties	4 (8.34)	Fear of being branded as party men	
Democracy	27 (56.75)	Any other	
Dictatorship	—	—	
Any other	—	—	

Political Activities During Student Days

The respondents were asked about their political activities in their student days

TABLE 40

Did You Engage in Any Political Activity as Student?

If yes, activities	*N*	*No active in*
Membership of student wing of political party	10(20%)	2(4%)
Taking part in rallies organized by the political parties	—	
Listening to speeches of important political leaders	22 (44%)	
Writing in newspapers or magazines on current political issues	14(28%)	
Taking part in debates, discussions and symposiums on current political issues	32 (625%)	
Full fledged membership of any political party	12(24%)	
Any other	—	

Ten (20%) respondents were members of student's wing of a political party as student. 14 (28%) wrote in newspapers and magazines on current political issues. Thirty-two (62%) have participated in debates, discussions and symposiums on current political issues, 22 (44%) have listened to speeches of important leaders while 12 (24%) have had full-fledged members of a Political Party as a student (Table 40).

Regular Member of Any Party at Present

The respondents were asked if they are a regular member of any party at present? All the respondents reported that they were regular members of Political Party, out of which 40 (80%) were active while 10 (20%) were passive members. The respondents were asked to name their party, and 20 (40%) were in Congress I while 14 (28%) were found to be members of Rashtriya Janata Dal, Five from B.J.P. and 4 from Samata Party. Regarding reasons for membership, 26 (52%) joined a particular party on the suggestion of others, while 10 (20%) were cajoled by the party and 8 were attracted by party programme (Table 41, 41.1 and 41.2).

TABLE 41

Are You a Regular Member of Any Political Party at Present?

Response	*Regular Member*	*Active Member*	*Passive Member*
Yes	50 (100%)	40 (80.00)	10 (20.00)
No	—	—	—
Total	**50 (100%)**		

TABLE 41.1

State the Name of the Party

Name of party	*N*	%
Congress	20	40.00
B.J.P.	5	10.00
R.J.D.	14	28.00
J.D.	1	2.00
Samajwadi Party	2	4.00
Samata Party	4	8.00
C.P.I.	1	2.00
C.P.M.	1	2.00
CPIML	-	
J.M.M.	1	2.00
J.P.P.	1	2.00
Total	**50**	**100.00**

TABLE 41.2

Reason of Membership

Reason	*N*	%
Personal benefit	1	2.00
Suggested by elder	26	52.00
Forced by party	10	20.00
Attracted by party programme	8	16.00
Influenced by the personality of the leader in party	3	6.00
Social work	2	4.00
Any other		
Total	**50**	**100.00**

The respondents were asked about their participation in party activities and 41 (82%) were participating while only 9 (18%) were not. 44 (88%) participated in processions, 28 (56%) in Demonstrations, 12 (24%) in Morchas and 25 in Morchas (Table 42 and 42.1).

TABLE 42

Do You Participate in the Activities of Any Party?

Response	*N*	%
Yes	41	82.00
No	9	18.00
Total	**50**	**100.00**

TABLE 42.1

What Activities

If yes	*N*	%
(A) Morcha	12	24.00
(B) Procession	44	88.00
(C) Demonstration	28	56.00
(D) Satyagrah		
(E) Political movement	25	50.00
Any other		

TABLE 43

Do You Have Any Political Aspiration?

Yes, political aspiration	*N*	%
Take to social work	32	64
Party work	10	20
Welfare of caste	4	8
Carrying favour of party leaders	4	8
Any other		
Total	**50**	**100**

The last question in this section asked them if they had any political aspirations and if yes, why? All the 50 respondents had this aspiration 64% aspired it for "social work", 20% to work for Party. 8% aspired for their own caste welfare, while 8% wanted to get the favour of their party leaders (Table 43).

The second section of Part IV of the schedule consists of questions armed at mapping the voting behaviour, their political career.

Voting

The respondents were given a set of reasons which made voting important for Democracy and they were asked to respond. 20 opined that voting is very important in a Democratic polity because this is the only Government which is of the people, for the people and by the people, 12 believed that voting is a reflection of peoples choice of their representatives. Eighteen respondents regarded it as very necessary for the working of Indirect Democracy (Table 44).

TABLE 44

Voting Behaviour is Important for Democracy

Why?	N	%
Democracy is the Govt. of the people for the people by the people	20	40
Voting indicates people's choice of their representatives	12	24
Voting is necessary in indirect Democracy	18	36
Any other	—	
Total	**50**	**100**

The respondents were asked next about their voting in any election and were also asked to name the year, Election and Party they had voted for the first time. All the respondents had voted sometime. Among the total 39 (78.00) had first voted for Lok Sabha while 11 (22.00) had first voted in Vidhan Sabha Elections. In Lok Sabha Elections, maximum of 10 voted for the first time in 1977 after 1952 Lok Sabha Elections in which ten had first voted. In 1952, 7 had voted for Congress while in 1977 five voted for the newly constituted Janata Party. In Vidhan Sabha Elections I had voted first time in '52. Three, the maximum, voted in 1985. Congress has had a fair share of votes (Table 45, 45.1, 45.2)

TABLE 45

State the Name of the Party

Response	*N*	*%*	*Lok Sabha*	*Vidhan Sabha*
Yes	50	100.00	39 (78.00)	11(22.00)
No	—	—	—	—
Total	**50**	**100.00**		

TABLE 45.1

Name First Election-Year and Party of Your Voting (Lok Sabha)

Year	*N*	*Party*
1957	10(25.64)	Congress-7, CPI-1, Socialist Party-2
1959	3 (7.69)	Congress-3
1962	2(5.13)	Congress-1, Socialist Party-1
1967	2(5.13)	JMM-1, Janata Party-1
1971	5(12.82)	Congress-4, Socialist- 1
1977	10(25.64)	Congress-4. JMM-1, JP-5
1980		
1984		
1989	2(5.13)	Janata Dal-2
1991	1 (2.56)	Congress- 1
1996	4(10.26)	Samata Party-1, CPI-1, JMM-2
Total	**39 (100.00)**	

TABLE 45.2

Name the Election Year and Party of First Voted in Vidhan Sabha Election

Year	*N*	*Party*
1957	1 (9.09)	Congress- 1
1972	1 (9.09)	Congress- 1
1980	2(18.18)	Lok Dal-1 , Congress-1
1985	3(27.28)	CPI-2, JD-1
1990	2(18.18)	Congress-2
1995	2(18.18)	BPP-1 , Congress- 1
Total	**11 (100.00)**	

Reasons for Voting

Thirty-two (64%) had voted on Party programme and manifesto, 12 on party, 2 were fascinated by the personality of the candidate, while 4 (8.00) had voted on caste considerations (Table 46).

TABLE 46

Reason for Voting

Reason	*N*	*%*
Fascinating personality	2	4
Party	12	24
Party programme, manifesto	32	64
Caste	4	8
Religion	—	
Suggested by other	—	
Forced by other	—	
Total	**50**	**100**

Voted in '98 and '95 Elections

In response to the next Question, 42 (84%) reported that they had voted in '98 Lok Sabha Elections, and only 8 (16.00) had obtained from voting. The maximum number had voted for Congress I, about 40.47% and 15 (35.71) had voted for R.J.D. (Table 47 and 47.1).

TABLE 47

Were You a Voter in 1998 Lok Sabha Election?

Response	*N*	%
Yes	42	84.00
No	8	16.00
Total	**50**	**100.00**

TABLE 47.1

If Yes—Name the Party

Party	*N*	%
BJP	2	4.76
Congress	17	40.47
R.J.D.	15	35.71
C.P.I.	1	2.38
C.P.M.	1	2.38
CPI ML		
J.D.	2	4.76
J.M.M.	2	4,76
Samata Party	2	4.76
Total	**42**	**100.00**

In '95 Vidhan Sabha (Bihar) elections 43 (86%) reported that they had voted while 7 had not. Here again the maximum number 18 (41.86) had voted for Congress while 15 (34.88) had voted for Janata Dal (Table 48 and 48.1)

TABLE 48

Were You a Voter in 1995 Bihar Vidhan Sabha Election?

Response	*N*	%
Yes	43	86.00
No	7	14.00
Total	**50**	**100.00**

TABLE 48.1

If yes, Name the Party

Name of the party	N	%
Congress	18	41.86
J.D.	15	34.88
J.M.M.	1	2.32
C.P.I	2	4.64
B.P.P	1	2.32
C.P.M	1	2.32
Samata Party	2	4.64
JPP	1	232
B.J.P.	2	4.64
Total	**43**	**100.00**

Canvassing for a Party

About 45 (90%) of the respondents had canvassed for Lok Sabha Elections while 30 (60%) had canvassed for Vidhan Sabha Elections. Maximum number had canvassed for Congress Party, from the earliest election. Canvassing was done also for J.D. and later on R.J.D. In the late 70's canvassing was done for Janata Party. The 80's and 90's saw canvassing for B.J.P. (Table 49 and 49.1).

TABLE 49

Did You Take Part in Canvassing for Any Party in the Elections?

	Lok Sabha		*Vidhan Sabha*	
Response	*N*	%	*N*	%
Yes	45	90	30	60
No	5	10	20	40
Total	**50**	**100**	**50**	**100**

TABLE 49.1

If Yes, Name the Year and Party

	Lok Sabha			*Vidhan Sabha*	
Year	*No*	*Party*	*Year*	*No*	*Party*
1952	5 (10.00)	Congress-4 Socialist- 1	1967	1 (2.00)	Congress
1957	5 (10.00)	Congress-4 Socialist-1	1969	2 (4.00)	Congress
1962	4 (8.00)	Congress	1972	2 (4.00)	Congress
1967	5 (10.00)	Congress	1977	1 (2.00)	Janata Party
1969	5 (10.00)	Congress-4 S.P.-1	1980	3 (6.00)	Congress
1971	4 (8.00)	Congress-3, S.P.-1	1985	2 (4.00)	Congress-1 C.P.M.-1
1977	6 (12.00)	JMM-1, JP-3, Congress-2	1990	5 (10.00)	JP-3, Congress-1 CPM-1
1980	9 (18.00)	JMM-1, JP-3, Lok Dal-1, Congress-3	1995	5 (10.00)	Samata Party-2 Ind.-1, JD-2
1989	7 (14.00)	Congress-1 JD-4, CPI-1 JP-1			
1991	7 (14.00)	BJP-1, CPM-1 Congress-3 JD-2			
1996	8 (16.00)	RJD-2, CPI-1, Samata Party-2 BJP-3			
1998	7 (14.00)	RJP-4, BJP-2 Samata Party-1			

Reasons for Canvassing

As regards reasons for canvassing for a party, 20 respondents were directed by the personality of the candidate while 18 did so because they liked the party programme. Seven canvassed because the candidate was related to them and four candidly put it-"For Fun" (Table 50)

TABLE 50

Reasons for Canvassing

Reasons	*N*	*%*
Party Programme	18	36
Personality of the candidate	20	40
Relation with candidate	7	14
Personal benefit	—	—
Religion	—	—
For fun	3	6
Any other	2	4
Total	**50**	**100**

The respondents were tested for their observation power during elections by identifying what elements operated during elections. 28 respondents observed the operation of caste and communal interests during elections, 18 observed groupism, 14 found "goonda elements" in operation, 22 observed extravagant display of money while 24 were witness to flexing of "muscle power" during elections (Table 51).

TABLE 51

Did You Notice the Following Elements Operating in the Elections?

Elements	*N*	*%*
Castism and communalism	28	56
Goondaism	14	28
Groupism	18	36
Extravagances of money	22	44
Use of muscle power	24	48
Any other	—	

Political Career History

All respondents accepted their desire for contesting elections on various grounds, 34 maintained that they were directed by their desire to serve people. Ten gave the most practical reason-power considerations; 6 respondents desired it for social prestige (Table 52).

TABLE 52

Do You Desire to Contest Election?

Yes, why	*N*	*No, why*	*N*
Desire to serve people	34 (68%)	Lack of funds	—
For power	10 (20%)	Apathy of political parties in gives ticket	—
For social prestige	6 (12%)	Increasing	—
Any other	—	Any other	—
Total	**50 (100.0)**	**Total**	—

The respondents were asked how many times they had contested elections? Six had contested Lok Sabha elections once and five had won. 17 had contested once for Vidhan Sabha and out of the total 15 (88.33) had won. Eight had contested twice for Lok Sabha, and five had won. In Vidhan Sabha 10 has contested twice and nine had won. One had contested for Lok Sabha three times and won while nine had contested for Vidhan Sabha out of which 5 had won. Eight had contested four times. Correspondingly 2, 3 and nine had won (Table 53).

TABLE 53

How Many Times You Have Contested Election as a Party Candidate?

	Lok Sabha			*Vidhan Sabha*		
	N	*W*	*Lost*	*N*	*W*	*%*
One Time	6	5 (83.33)	1 (16.67)	17	15 (88.33)	2 (11.77)
Two time	8	5 (62.5)	3 (37.5)	10	9 (90.0)	1 (10.0)
Three time	1	1 (100.0)		9	5 (55.55)	4 (44.45)

(Contd.)

(Contd. Table 53)

Four time	8	4 (50.0)	4 (50.0)	3	2 (66.67)	3 3 (33.33)
Five time	10	6 (60.0)	4 (40.0)	5	3 (60.0)	2 (40.0)
Five time above	6	1 (16.67)	5 (83.33)	18	9 (50.0)	9 (50.0)

The respondents were asked if they had ever served in the Union Cabinet and State Council of Ministers? According to the responses, 13 out of 50 had served in either Union Cabinet or State Council of Ministers, or in both. Two had served as Minister of State in the Union Cabinet, namely Tarkeshwari Sinha and Krishna Shahi. Tarkeshwari Sinha had first served as Deputy Minister of State. At the State level, 2 had served as Cabinet Minister for one term, one for two terms and three for 2 terms. Eight had served minister of State in council of Ministers for one term while 2 had served for 2 terms, Two respondents had served once as Deputy Minister of State in Bihar Council of Ministers (Table 54 and 54.1). (See list of Ministers in Bihar Council of Ministers in Appendix).

TABLE 54

Have You Ever Served in the Council of Ministers at Centre and State Level?

Response	*N*	*%*
Yes	13	26.00
No	37	74.00
Total	**50**	**100.00**

TABLE 54.1

Have You Ever Served in the Council of Ministers of Centre and State Level? If Yes, How Many Times?

	Centre			*State*		
	Cabinet	*State*	*Deputy*	*Cabinet*	*State*	*Deputy*
One Time		2	1	2	8	2
Two Time				1	2	
Three Time				2		

Change of Party Membership

The respondents were asked if they had changed their party membership ever. Twenty-one respondents accepted to changing their party membership. 29 respondents had changed their party membership on various grounds listed-nine had changed party due to rift in party while 7 changed because of the declining esteem of the party. 2 changed party due to the electoral failure of the party, two due to their desire to win election while one changed party due to changes in the party ideology (Table 55, 55.1, 55.2).

TABLE 55

Have You Ever Changed Your Party Membership?

Response	*N*	%
Yes	21	42.00
No	29	58.00
Total	**50**	**100.00**

TABLE 55.1

If Yes, Name the Year, Old Party and New Party

Year	*No*	*Old Party*	*New Party*
1969	1	Congress	Congress I
1995	1	Congress I	Samata Party.
1996	3	Janata Dal-3 Samajwadi Party-1	Congress I-1 RJD-1, Ind-1
1997	7	JD-5 Congress-1 JMM-1	RJD-6 JPP-1
1998	9	JD-4 Congress I-5	RJD-6 Jan Congress-2 Samata Party-1
Total	**21**		

TABLE 55.2

If yes, Reason	*N*	%
(i) Change in Party ideology	1	1.38
(ii) Rift in party	9	12.43
(iii) Failure of the party in elections	2	2.76
(iv) Desire to win in election	2	2.76
(v) Low esteem of the party	7	9.67
Total	**21**	**29.00**

The respondents were asked their opinion about Anti Defection Law. As we all know, defection has become a common practice especially during "election season" to ensure electoral success. 32 respondents expressed their approval of this law, while eighteen respondents expressed their disapproval.

1. To check corruption by 12 (37.5%
2. To develop party discipline 8 (25%)
3. For stability of the Government 8 (25%)
4. Check on opportunist politics 4(12.25%)

Those who disapproved of Anti-Defection Law gave their own reason. Seven believe that fear of defection puts a check on the arbitrariness of party leaders while 2 believed that the inner atmosphere of any party will become more open and democratic. Eight opined that defection gives the second rank political leaders a chance to go up higher in politics by organizing another party, or joining some other party, on his/her terms (Table 56 and 56.1).

TABLE 56

Do You Approve of Anti-Defection Law?

Response	*N*	%
Yes	32	64
No	18	36
Total	**50**	**100**

TABLE 56.1

If yes, why	*N (%)*	*If no, why?*	*N (%)*
To check corruption in politics	12 (37.5)	It will check arbitrariness of party leadership	7 (38.89)
To develop party discipline	8 (25.00)	Second rank leaders will get a chance to go up in political hierarchy	8 (49.99)
Stability of Government	8 (25.0)	More democracy within the party	2 (11.10)
Check on opportunity politics	4 (12.25)	Any other	1 (5.55)
Total	**32**	**Total**	**18**

For the last two decades defection from one party to other on the floor of the Lok Sabha and Assemblies has become a common political scene. Governments are toppled, and there is no stability. The years between 1990 to present 2001 have witnessed several such incidents making the governments instable and putting the general public to the hardships of frequent elections. The response to this question should have been unanimous approval, but it is not so.

TABLE 57

Do You Believe that Party Support is Necessary for Contesting Election?

If yes, reasons	*N*	*%*
Party provides a platform	10	20
Gives publicity	12	24
Party strength	16	32
Influences the electorate in favour	8	16
Provides funds	4	8
Any other	—	
Total	**50**	**100**

The respondents were asked whether support of any political party was necessary for contesting election. All the respondents agreed that party support was necessary because of various reasons. 16 believed that the strength of the party was a big support. Twelve opined that party provided publicity to the candidate while 10 thought that party provided a 'Platform'. Eight agreed that party could influence the voters in favour of the candidates and four realized the financial help given by the party (Table 57).

The last Question put to the respondents was regarding their opinion towards 33% reservation for women in Lok Sabha and State Legislatures. Forty-three respondents were in favour of reservations. Twenty-three among them believed that the increased number of women in Lok Sabha could ensure the entry of problem issues related to women in the house, and remedial measures could be decided in Lok Sabha. Fifteen maintain that reservation will make elections easy for women, because more women will get election tickets and the constituency will be reserved for women 3 believed that parties will be forced to give tickets to women and two felt that the presence of women in Lok Sabha will be more visible.

TABLE 58

What is Your Reaction Towards 33% Reservation for Women

If agree, why	*N*	*If disagree, why*	*N*
It will make easy for women to fight election	15 (34.88)	It is against the principles of Democracy	—
Parties will be forced to put up women candidate	3 (6.97)	Benefit elite class	4 (57.14)
Their present in the Lok Sabha and Vidhan Sabha will be felt	2 (4.65)	Problem of the common women will not be highlighted	2 (28.56)
They will bring up problems of women in these Sabha and forced remedies	23 (53.49)	It will affect smooth working of the Sabha	
		Because most of the women will be in-experienced	1 (14.29)
		Any other	
Total	**43 (100.0)**	**Total**	**7 (100.0)**

Seven respondents did not favour reservation. 4 opined that it will benefit only elite women, while two believed that the problems of common women will not be highlighted. One respondent believed that the women coming through reservation will mostly be inexperienced (Table 58).

A few respondents were taken up for case history and in-depth interviews were conducted with them.

Tarkeshwari Sinha

Tarkeshwari Sinha is one of the oldest member of Bihar Vidhan Sabha, Lok Sabha and has also served as Deputy Minister Finance and Minister of State for Finance for nearly six years (1958-1964) in the Union Cabinet. She has been a veteran parliamentarian and fire-brand politician in the mid 50's and 60's. She was given a portfolio as important as Finance. Talking to her one felt that she still had that 'fire' inside her. She was frank in her assessment of the present political scenario. She maintained that in the earlier days after Independence politicians were dedicated towards ideals, more committed to "public good". Today it was a total mess, with increasing use of 'violence' and "money power". The politicians were self-seekers. Tarkeshwari Sinha is an M.Sc. from London School of Economics and has had good education. She participated first in 1942 movement as a student and was imprisoned. She has been active in Politics from her student days. Unlike many others, entering politics was her own decision. She won general elections from 1952 to 1967. She lost in 1971 after joining Congress I in 1969. The advent of Indira Gandhi on the political horizon of India proved fatal for Tarkeshwari Sinha. In 1964 she decided to leave "electoral politics" for ever. She maintained that she did not want to participate any more in elections with the help of 'dirty' political stunts and muscle power. She has supported 33% reservation for women.

Uma Pandey

Uma Pandey has played an important role in Bihar Politics since 1957. She fought elections on Congress Party's ticket for eight times and lost three times—in 1969, 1977 and 1990. With Congress loosing ground in Bihar she has not been able to win any election after 1985. She has been cabinet rank minister in

Bihar Council of Ministers three times (till 1989 end) and wielded such important portfolios as Education, Revenue, Labour. She has also been chairperson of Public Accounts Committee and Estimates Committee, Bihar Vidhan Sabha. She changed her party from Congress I to Bihar Jan Congress in 1998, but she did not win the following elections.

Known for her efficiency integrity and honesty she has had a long innings in politics. She has been out of power due to party politics in Bihar. She had entered politics at the tender age of 25 on the advice of her husband and remained in power for almost three and a half decades. Her services could still be important for the State, given a chance. She represents the category of well-educated and cultured politicians. She whole-heartedly supported the issue of 33% reservation for women. She wants politics to be free of caste considerations. For her caste is the root cause of corruption in Bihar Politics. She is very much in favour of Anti-defection law. She may not be in power politics now but she has clear views and still believes in the role of ideology in Politics.

Prabhawati Gupta

Prabhawati Gupta has been contesting elections since 1952 regularly and winning. In 1984 she won the Lok Sabha Election. She lost just once, in 1962. She was State Minister for Finance, Transport, Mines since 1973-1980 in Bihar and Cabinet Minister Labour in 1983-84 after which she went to the Centre as member of Parliament. She was a member of Public Accounts Committee and Public Undertakings Committee of Lok Sabha. She represented India in International Labour Organisation in Geneva in 1984. She was also made a member of a delegation of Lok Sabha to the European Parliaments meeting at Strasburg of France.

She believes in the equality of men and women. She supports 33% reservation for women in strong words. Prabhawati Gupta comes from a very family oriented background, yet she has performed well in various capacities in Politics. She is a well read and much traveled person. She also represents the generation which was well educated, committed to work and believed in some ideology in Politics.

Krishna Shahi

Krishna Shahi comes from a very well known political family. She is the daughter of Late Mahesh Prasad Sinha, one of the earliest most important Congress leaders after Sri Krishna Singh. One could say that Ms Shahi has literally learned about 'politics' in her father's lap. However she entered electoral politics rather late—at the age of 36 years; and was influenced by her husband who himself was an I.P.S. Officer. She has a B.A. and LL.B. degree. She first fought for Vidhan Sabha elections in 1972, and again in 1977 and won. In 1980 and 1984 she won Lok Sabha elections and had a stint of two terms in the Parliament. Later on she again won in '91 and remained in M.P. till '96. She was the only Congress M.P. elected from Bihar in '97. She has been a vocal parliamentarian. She was State Minister for Education and Culture, and Water Resources and Culture from 1986-1989. Earlier she had also served in the capacity of Chairperson Patna Regional Development Authority 1976-77 and Improvement Trust-1970-74. She has been a member of Senate and Syndicate of Bihar and Patna University.

Reputed once as a Congress contestant who won with the highest number of votes in several elections from Begusarai she still desires to contest elections. But now she has decided not to enter electoral politics until it is made free of anti-social elements.

However, she is against 33% reservation for women because for her it is going against the principles of Democracy. She also maintains that it will not benefit common women.

Much traveled and sophisticated, Krishna Shahi is a typical women politician whose family had a lot to contribute to her career. She is out and out an example of "elite political women" with little connection with the grass-root people.

Sushila Kerketta

Sushila Kerketta comes from tribal background, and has performed very well both as a member of Vidhan Sabha and also as a Minister. She holds a Masters degree, and came into politics from teaching profession. She entered politics at the age of 30 years and made the decision herself. She does not have any member of her family in politics. She fought Vidhan Sabha elections in 1985 and 1990, 1995 and won in all three. She lost Lok Sabha elections in 1996 and 1998. She was Minister of State for Irrigation in Bihar from 1985-88. She was cabinet rank minister for Food and Civil Supply, Commerce and Rural Development from March '89 to December '89. She was cabinet minister for Mines and Geology from December '89 to March '90. She did not come back as M.L.A. in 2000 Vidhan Sabha Election. She was the deputy leader of Congress Legislative Party in 1998 and Chair of Jharkhand Regional Congress. She has been Principal of Birsa College Khunti, Sushila Kerketta has been legislator for three terms in Bihar Vidhan Sabha, and served as minister for two to three terms. She has represented her Tribal Community very well, and supports 33% reservation for women strongly.

Sudha Srivastava

Sudha Srivastava is the product of Jai Prakash Narain's Total Revolution movement in Bihar and fought Vidhan Sabha Elections for the first time in 1977 on Janata Party ticket and won. She lost in 1980 and won again in 1990 on Janata Party ticket. She also became cabinet rank minister for Health in 1990 and continued till July 1994. She is the only lady politician who resigned from her post due to ideological differences with the then Chief Minister of Bihar, Laloo Prasad Yadav.

From the present lot, Kanti Singh shot to fame by winning Lok Sabha Elections in 1996 on Janata Dal ticket. She was also made State level minister for Coal in the Centre in 1996. She lost in '98 but won again in '99. Shanti Devi, Sita Sinha, Abo Devi have been ministers in Bihar Council of Minister several times from '90 onwards. All belonged to earlier Janata Dal and later Rashtriya Janata Dal. Sita Sinha and Kanti Singh have been College teachers before joining politics. Kanti Singh has a doctoral degree too. They have joined active politics in the early age group of 30-35 years.

The respondents in this category are definitely more active and aware of Politics. They have been/ are active participants, and served in various categories. Most of them have repeated their electoral success several times and served especially in the Council of Ministers in Bihar for several terms such as Uma

Pandey, Prabhawati Gupta, Sushila Kerketta and in recent decade Shanti Devi, Abo Devi, Sita Sinha. Tarkeshwari was Deputy Minister of State for Finance in the Centre from 1958-66. Krishna Shahi was minister of State for Education and Culture in the Centre from 1984-86.

Tarkeshwari Sinha excelled herself as a Parliamentarian while Uma Pandey, Prabhawati Gupta and others have been very vocal legislators in Bihar and able and efficient ministers several times. However the influence of the family is very much there. There are only isolated cases of women politicians who decided to join politics on their own such as Tarkeshwari Sinha and Sushila Kerketta. Most of them have had family members in active politics before coming into politics, such as Krishna Shahi whose father was one of the top most earlier leaders of Congress in Bihar, Kanti Singh has a brother in Politics.

The number and percentage of women from Bihar in Lok Sabha has been very small, but most of them did make a mark by their presence there. In the Bihar Vidhan Sabha the percentage of women was impressive in first two three elections but declined sharply to finally become steady between 10-13. The present Vidhan Sabha, however, has nineteen women legislators.

The respondents have identified caste as the bane of politics in Bihar. Some earlier women political leaders have decided to avoid "electoral politics" because of growing criminalisation of politics—use of money and muscle power and lack of ideology.

On the current important issue of 33% reservation for women, most of the respondents have supported it. Similarly a good percentage of respondents support Anti-defection Law because it would make the government stable.

The self perception of the respondents is by and large very positive and mostly they believe that men and women should have equal status, nature has not made men superior. It is the society which gives prominence to the male.

8

Conclusion and Recommendations

The findings of the Research Project on "Empowerment of Women through Political Participations: A Study of Women's political participation in Bihar" are very significant. The findings confirm that the low socio-economic and educational status of women in Bihar has affected to a great extent the participation of women in politics. The hold of 'Patriarchy' on political institutions is confirmed by the finding. The findings also support the hypothesis that the general culture of violence in Bihar, and the acute criminalisation of politics prevents women's entry into politics. They are hesitant to perform their duty even as voters because of Poll Violence. Lack of education and employment is a deterrent in the development of a positive image of the self in women. Also, the age-old feudal values which have placed women in a secondary position in the society, still hold women captive. They are hesitant about a full-time political career for women, and the arguments given by them are age-old arguments. The responses vary from category to category of respondents. For example, the responses from the category of women political decision-makers are more clear and positive. They have been regular voters, members of Political Parties and taken part in various party activities. They also have by and large, a positive image of the self. On the other hand, the housewives (120) from the Voters' category have given poor response to questions addressed to them to gauze their aptitude and awareness of politics. Many of them have never voted or taken part in canvassing. In comparison, the professionals (80) from the 'Voters' category have given a much better response. They have a more positive perception of the 'self. They understand the importance of education and full time job for creating more confidence in them. In between the two categories of Voters' and 'Political decision-makers' are the categories of 'Political Activists' and of those who never won elections. The respondents in 'Activists' category have given good responses to the questions addressed to them. Their confidence is praiseworthy, and their range of activities is good. Yet electoral success has eluded them. Nevertheless, this category represents the breeding ground for future legislators. As has happened in the case of or Sukhada Pandey, our respondent in this category, who got elected to the Bihar Vidhan Sabha between the period of data collection in 98-99 and the writing of this report. On the other hand some hard-core activists like Saroj Chaube could not win a single election. The last category is a "mutely crowd" of hard-core, well cultivated party activists on the one hand and total novices on the other hand, who have neither worked in public life, nor they know the a.b.c. of politics.

Following are the conclusions drawn from the responses of the respondents, information and interviews regarding crucially important issues related to women's political participation:

Perception of the Self

The data reveals that not many have a positive image of the self (women) out of the total sample of 350, as many as 235 (67.14%) do not accept that women enjoy an equal status with men in real life. Five (1.42%) have given no response. One hundred and forty respondents nearly 40% of the total do not believe in the natural superiority of men over women, but 194 (55.42%) accept that men are by nature superior to women. This is an indication of the low esteem women have about themselves. Consciously or subconsciously, women are apt to consider men superior to women. Even the respondents from the decision-makers, activists and contestants who never won categories have not expressed a very positive image of the 'self.'

However, the importance of education in the cultivation of positive image of women has been encouragingly accepted. Out of 350, 335 (95.71) have supported education for women. About

186 (53.14) have supported graduate level education for women. The responses also reveal that about 326 (93.14) regard the status of educated women as superior to uneducated women.

The importance of full time job or career has been accepted as a major factor contributing towards the building up of confidence in the self. 251 (71.71) accept that full-time career gives confidence, self-confidence does pave the way for "positive" image of the self.

Political Aptitude and Awareness

The responses to the questions put to the respondents to measure their political aptitude amplify that 178 (50.85) were in favour of political career for women, and as many as 219 (62.57) had faith that women would be successful in political leadership positions. Thus women are inclined towards "Politics", if they are against it or doubtful about their success in leadership position, it is due to the hold of traditional values—that it will break the family, damage their image, and their temperament is not suited to political career. On the other hand, increasing criminalisation and violence in politics, excessive use of money and muscle power deters women from their desire to take part in politics.

Political Awareness

The responses reveal that the respondents are fairly aware of politics. They have correctly identified political leaders of national level and in Bihar. The national and regional political parties have been named correctly to a large extent. The pattern of Indian government has been identified quite well.

Indira Gandhi, Sarojini Naidu, Vijayalaxmi Pandit have been named as national political leader by the majority while in the second place are the names of Sonia Gandhi, Sushama Swaraj and Tarkeshwari Sinha. In Bihar Rabri Devi has been named by maximum number of respondents. Next come Rita Verma and Kanti Singh, while old timer Uma Pandey has been mentioned by a very good number.

Gandhi and Nehru have been identified by almost 90% of the respondents as important political leaders of the world. Lal Bahadur Shastri and, Jai Prakash Narain also enjoy the support of good number of respondents. Laloo Yadav has been identified by more than 90% respondents as the political leader of Bihar. Next come Ram Vilas Paswan, Jagannath Mishra and Karpoori Thakur. A good number have also mentioned K.B. Sahay.

293 (83.71) among the total respondents have correctly identified the pattern of Indian Government as Parliamentary form of government. 336 (96%) respondents have correctly named Rashtriya Janata Dal as the Ruling Party in Bihar, while 330 (94.28) have named B.J.P. as the main Opposition Party in Bihar.

Opinion is directed on the importance of caste in Bihar Politics, 149 (42.57) regard caste as the bane of politics in Bihar, while 146 (49.71) negate it. As many as 55 (15.71) did not give any response.

In evaluating politics of Bihar, 173 (49.42) regard it as totally corrupt. As regards the creation of a separate Jharkhand State, the responses of nearly 199 (56.85) have been proved wrong. They were against a separate Jharkhand State. As we all know, the state has come into existence on 15.11.2000.

In a nutshell, the respondents have a good awareness of the political system in India and Bihar. Among all the categories of respondents, the category of Political decision-maker and Activists displays maximum awareness, while in the 'Voters' category the "Professionals" are much more aware politically, than the housewives.

Participation in Politics—Voting and Contesting Elections

The responses reveal that 280 respondents (80%) have voted in elections. In 1998 Lok Sabha Elections 263 (75.14%) have taken part as Voters while in '95 Bihar Vidhan Sabha Elections 241 (68.85%) voted. This is an indicator that a very good per cent of respondents have voted in elections. In the 'Voters' category 130 out of 200 did take part in voting, which is very 'high' percentage. As we have seen, voting in '98 Lok Sabha Elections and '95 Bihar Vidhan Sabha elections also has been very satisfactory. One can conclude that as far as voting is concerned, the respondents in our sample have done a good job.

Unfortunately, the same cannot be said about 'Canvassing

Out of the total, only 157 (44.85%) had taken part in canvassing while 193 (55.14%) had not. In the voter category only 20 had done canvassing.

One can conclude here that though women have increased their participation as voters, they still suffer from inhibitions in participating in other activities. The family by and large does not support the idea of the women walking door to door for canvassing. Not a single 'housewife' respondent has taken part in canvassing.

Contesting Elections

The conclusion drawn from the responses is that 169 (48.28%) did desire to contest elections for various reasons. Out of the total 100 (MLA, MP + those who never won) maximum had fought elections on party ticket. About 22 in the category of contestants who never did win, fought as Independents.

The respondents do realize the importance of the support of a political party for entering electoral politics. In the MLA, MP categories all are regular members of some political parties. Majority of those who are or have been members of Parliament or Vidhan Sabha have won on Congress I and R.J.D. ticket. During the Janata' wave in 70's, women won on Janata Dal ticket. Left parties have not put up good number of candidates. Their electoral success has been few and far between. Congress Party has been the largest promoter of women in election process.

Women Political Decision-makers

In this category about thirteen (26%) have served as Ministers at the Union Cabinet and/or State Council of Ministers. Twenty-four are/ have been members of Bihar Vidhan Sabha, 10 are/have been members of Lok Sabha.

The number as per the records is small and so is it in the sample. Although there have been lady politicians with very good education, honesty, integrity, and intellect, only a few have been able to become ministers. A good many have performed their duties excellently such as Tarkeshwari Sinha, Ramdulari Sinha, Krishna Shahi and at present, Rita Verma. Similarly, Bihar has given fiery and capable women parliamentarians. The picture, of course, is not that bright when one comes to State Politics.

However, women ministers in 50's to 80's did a good job. Some coming from R.J.D. are also doing well.

Party Membership and Participation in Party Activities

Out of 150 respondents in the three categories who are active in politics, 113 (75.34%) are regular members of some political party. About 109 are very active members. The MLA, MPs and ministers are/have been active members of some political party. Nearly 146 (97.34%) believe that party support is necessary to contest and win elections. They have hit the crucial point that without the support of party, it is difficult to win elections. If parties are apathetic towards women it is difficult to increase their number in legislative and decision-making bodies.

About 50 among the 150 have been regular members of the student's wing of some political party and have participated in various activities of the party. The response however reveals that about 110 respondents of these categories have not been associated with parties during their student days. One may conclude that a very small percentage of girls in Bihar are closely associated with any political party as students unlike some other states.

Seventy-four out of 150 respondents have changed their membership sometime or other for various reasons such as split in the party, electoral debacle of the party, apathy of the party in giving ticket to women candidates, and sometimes, change in ideology.

Hurdles to Women's Entry Into Politics

Following hurdles in the path of women's meaningful entry and participation in politics can be identified through the responses of the respondents:

1. *Apathy of Political Parties*— Ten out of 50 in "Activists" category blamed the apathy of the political parties, for not desiring to contest elections. Similarly among those who contested but never won, many pin-pointed this factor. Twenty-two had contested elections as Independents and lost because they were denied 'ticket' from their party. By and large, the political parties are very reluctant to put up female candidates for election. Only

the Congress Party has tried to put women for 10% of the total seats to be contested by it.

2. *Lack of Funds*— Women do not have funds for fighting elections. If the party does not support them, they are just unable to contest elections and if they do, they loose almost always. Lack of funds has been identified as a major factor by the 'Activists' and contestants who never won. Thus, women even though they desire, are hesitant to enter the election process as contestants.

3. *Excessive use of money and muscle power*— Excessive use of money and muscle-power for winning election is a great deterrent towards women fighting elections only such women can choose to fight elections who have support of the party funds, or family funds and male-relatives who can manage both—money and muscle power.

4. *Culture of Violence during elections*— Violence during 'polling' is a factor which prevents women from exercising their voting rights. Booth capturing, snatching of ballot paper, bomb-explosions, firing are some of the recurring features of election scenario in Bihar, which discourage women from performing their primary political right and duty—voting! Unless the law and order situation is rigorously maintained and women voters are given special protection while exercising their 'Franchise' the turnout of women-voters is never going to be very high.

5. *The role of patriarch is still very dominant*— The decision to enter politics is rarely made by women themselves. It is made by their male relatives specifically father and/or husband. Sixty-four (42.67%) out of the 150 respondents joined politics due to the influence of their father while 56 (37.34%) were influenced by their husbands to join politics. Taken together 120 (80%) were influenced by their male relatives. Fathers of 25 (16.6%) and husbands of 60 (40%) are/or were in politics. The patriarch also decides the voting choices of the women of the family, their party membership and finally their desire to contest elections. This magnitude of dependency on the male can hardly help women to find and establish their own identity in politics. Their entry itself is not possible.

Further this patriarchal control finds its expression in party 'leadership' which is almost always male. The same bias persists. Women if allowed to 'enter' are kept in the 'periphery' of political arena.

These are the hurdles identified by the respondents. These hurdles need to be removed and a more congenial socio-political environment conducive to women's meaningful presence and participation in Politics has to be created. However, it is easily said than done. In a state like Bihar which is plagued by feudal traditions, low urbanization, lowest literacy ratio of women in India, poverty, politicization of caste and criminalisation of politics, it is a 'Herculean' task.

Yet, we have to make an effort to improve the situation. Women's participation, and a viable one, is not only necessary for Bihar, but also for the country. Bihar does play and has played a crucial role for the last four decades in national politics. Women of Bihar have participated in a massive scale in political movements. It is time they made their mark in structural politics and processes at the state and national level as well.

The remedial measures need to be classified in two categories —Immediate, and Long time. Long term measures are continuous processes to cure a very old and ill society, as Bihar has. The illness lies in a myriad of historical, social, economic, cultural and political factors which cannot be 'wished' away overnight. So, such measures have to continue for a long time to come, and should have a long range. But to avert the crisis of the present some immediate measures are urgently needed.

Recommendations: Short-term Measures

1. The most popular demand in the air at present is for 33% reservation for women in the Legislative bodies from the centre to the local level institutions. The 73rd Amendment to the Constitution in 1992 made provisions for 33% reservation for women in Panchayati Raj local institutions from district to the village level. Unfortunately the Bill for 33% reservation for women in Lok Sabha and State Assemblies has been caught in rough weather ever since its introduction through 81st Amendment 1996, which has not been passed as yet. It has been caught in

the web of controversies. It is high time that a consensus was evolved and reservation for women be provided in Lok Sabha and State Assemblies, at least for one decade.

2. Lack of funds is a great hurdle in the way of women's entry into electoral politics. Therefore. some sort of mechanism needs to be Developed for providing funds to the female aspirants. State funding of elections is an issue which has been a topic of debate for quite sometime. May be, a start could be made by at least providing state funding for women contestants. Some sort of 'revolving fund' needs to be evolved. The Election Commission could give serious thought to this issue and direct the State Government and Election Commission Bihar to do the needful.
3. Stringent measures need to be taken to ensure a violence-free atmosphere during elections. It is a known fact that incidents of violence—booth capturing, firing, goondaism eve-teasing are initiated by politicians. Strict measures should be taken against such politicians and contestants who through their money and muscle-power want to ensure their electoral victory. The Election Commission should devise measures to cancel the election of such contestants who indulge in violent activities during elections. The State Administration should exercise extra caution and take strict measures to control and ensure peaceful elections.
4. The Election Commission of India should give serious thought to devising some measures to ensure that the Political Parties are compelled to put up a good percentage of women candidates, at least 33% of the total candidates set up by any Party. This point has been emphasized in the "Platform of Action" at the World Congress of women at Beijing in 1995. In the last five years, Political Parties in various countries have adopted quota system for women while contesting elections, and it has made a considerable change, and increased the "visibility" of women in legislative bodies. A consensus should be evolved by the important Political Parties through

meetings, debates and discussions. The Election Commission should find ways and means to compel the Political Parties to take this measure for ensuring women's entry into electoral politics.

5. Politics in Bihar has been totally criminalized. Criminals are given tickets to fight elections. Political murders of candidates is the order of the day. There is a code of ethics for conduct of elections, but it is often observed in negation. The State Government, the State Election Commission should be carefully monitored by the centre, and those who are found guilty should be severely punished.
6. The judiciary has to play a very dynamic role in preventing the grant of 'ticket' by Political Parties to candidates for election who have even the slightest record of indulgence in criminal activities. If some one is in prison on criminal charges, it should be taken as sufficient reason for barring such people from contesting elections. Also, any aspirant who has a record of committing violence against women such as rape, murder, abduction, should be debarred from fighting elections.

Long Term Measures

Women in Bihar suffer from a very low socio-economic and educational status. It is a result of centuries of oppression, the hold of patriarchy and feudal values which have relegated women to a secondary position in the society, and that too, a very "poor second"! Society in Bihar has not changed much in the last half century, and it would be a "wishful dream" to expect it to change overnight. But the pace of change and progress needs to be accelerated in right earnest-priorities are very clear. The need of the hour is to take up "massive rebuilding operations" so as to improve the overall status of women in Bihar which can further ensure the meaningful political participation of women:-

1. Spread of literacy—A massive campaign for female literacy needs to be launched with a tight time-bound target to make women in Bihar literate. It has to be taken like a 'mission' and non governmental organizations with a

clean record, integrity and dedication should be involved to spread literacy among women in Bihar. The Government of Bihar should make it a priority area with 'enough funds' and also ensure that programmes are executed properly to yield good results. Continuous monitoring of such programmes needs to be done. The Government of India should extend cooperation and control in the execution of such programmes. Universal Secondary School level education should be the top-most priority, and later more and more seats should be added for women in technical/professional courses such as medicine, engineering, computer's etc. Functional literacy is important for all but very very important for women. The pace of the programmes for functional literacy should be accelerated and given priority.

2. Employment generation programmes for women. There are certain areas of work where women should be given topmost-priority such as Primary School Teaching, nursing, tele-communications, Public relations media related jobs. The Government should start some sort of policy of "positive discrimination" in making placements in technical jobs in favour of women.

3. There has been a spurt in crimes against women and girls in the last one and a half decade. It is necessary to devise mechanism for security of women and girls in educational institutions, work place, in public places, traveling etc. culprits should be immediately brought to task, whatever their connections may be. A consensus needs to be developed for introducing "capital punishment" for "rapists", "imprisonment" and "very heavy fines" for even teasers, abductors. Further, caste gang-wars need to be controlled, because women are the worst victims in such caste-wars.

4. Massive programmes needs to be continuously in operation for some decades to come, to create political aptitude and awareness among women. This is the area where the government needs to involve more and more NGO's and voluntary organisations. Women need to be

given "political information"; information about their government, the governmental policies, their achievements and failures Some sort of information given by political parties during elections through meetings, door-to-door campaigns, pamphlets, and election-manifesto is not enough. It has to be given continuously and made a important part of women's thinking and behaviour pattern.

5. Training in political activities needs to be imparted to women through camps in a continuous process. It should be made a part of student's extra-curricular activities at school and college level. The Government should make it a part of the education policy. Again, the cooperation of non-governmental organistion should be sought for this stupendous task.
6. Last but not the least, a change in the socialization process of girls needs to be brought about They should be 'taught' about their "true worth" from their very childhood. For this, educated parents are needed or awareness programmes for the parents needs to be launched. They play a very important role in giving "correct values" to their children. Values of gender equality need to be cultivated in the family from the very childhood stage. Later on, educational institutions can take this process further ahead

A crusade against feudal values of male domination over the female needs to be undertaken through debates, discussions, media, starting of course, from the family. Spread of education, opportunities of work, rapid urbanisation can slacken the hold of "feudal values" over the life of women

A continuous process of social, economic and political reconstruction needs to be started and carried on in right earnest, if things are to change for better. In this gigantic task all need to join hands—the society, the government, the voluntary organizations, the men and of course the women themselves! Then only can one expect the true empowerment of women!

Appendices

APPENDIX-1-CHAPTER-1

List of Women MP's from Bihar

Year	*Name*	*Party*
1957	Smt. Tarkeshwari Sinha	Congress
	Smt Shakuntala Devi	Congress
	Smt Satyabhama Devi	Congress
	Smt I lita Rajyalaxmi	Janta Party of Ramgarh House
	Smt Vijaya Raje	Janta Party of Ramgarh House
1962	Smt Tarkeshwari Sinha	Congress
	Smt Shakuntala Devi	Congress
	Smt Satyabhama Devi	Congress
	Smt Ram Dulari Sinha	Congress
	Smt Lalita Rajyalaxmi	Swatantra Party
	Smt Vijaya Raje	Swatantra Party
	Smt Shashank Manjari	watantra Party
1967	Smt Tarkeshwari Sir'	Congress
	Sushri Kamala Kumari	Congress
	Smt Lalita Rajyalaxmi	Independent
	Smt Vijaya Raje	Independent
1971	Sushri Kamala Kumari	Congress
1977	Nil	
1980	Smt. Ramdulari Sinha	Congress
	Smt. Krishna Shahi	Congress
	Smt. Madhuri Singh	Congress
	Sushri Kamala Kumari	Congress
	Smt. Kishori Sinha	Janta Dal
	Smt. Sumati Oraon	

1984	Smt. Prabhawati Gupta	Congress
	Smt. Kishori Sinha	Congress-I
	Smt. Ram Dulari Sinha	INC
	Smt. Chandra Bhanu Devi	INC
	Smt. Madhuri Singh	INC
	Smt. Manorama Singh	INC
	Smt. Krishna Shahi	INC
	Smt. Sumati Oraon	INC
	Sushri Kamala Kumari	
1989	Smt. Usha Singh	Janata Dal
	Smt. Sumati Oraon	Congress I
1991	Smt. Krishna Shahi	Congress
	Smt. Rita Verma	BJP
	Smt. Girija Pandey	Janata Dal
1996	Smt. Rita Verma	BJP
	Smt. Kanti Singh	Janata Dal
	Smt. Bhagwati Devi	Janata Dal
1998	Smt. Rita Verma	BJP
	Smt. Abha Mahato	BJP
	Smt. Malati Devi	RJD
1999	Smt. Rita Verma	BJP
	Smt. Abha Mahato	BJP
	Smt. Renu Kumari	JDU
	Smt. Shyama Singh	Congress
	Smt. Kanti Singh	RJD

Source: General Elections to Lok Sabha-Statistical Analysis. Reports of Election Commission, New Delhi.

APPENDIX-II-CHAPTER-1

List of Women Winner-Bihar Vidhan Sabha Elections from 1952 Onwards

Sl. No.	*Name*	*Party*
	1952	
1.	Smt. Sarswati Choudhary	Congress
2.	Smt. Sundari Devi	Congress
3.	Smt. Manorama Devi	Congress
4.	Smt. Sumitra Devi	Congress
5.	Smt. Ramswarupa Devi	Congress
6.	Smt. Parwati Devi	Congress
7.	Smt. Prabhawati Gupta	Congress
8.	Smt. Ram Dulari Sinha	Congress
9.	Smt. Krishna Devi	Congress
10.	Smt. Janak Kishori Devi	Congress
11.	Smt. Jyotirmayee Devi	Congress
12.	Smt. Manorama Sinha	Independent
	1957	
13.	Smt. Ketaki Devi	Congress
14.	Smt. Shakuntala Devi Agrawal	Congress
15.	Smt. Prabhawati Gupta	Congress
16.	Smt. Anusuiya Devi	Congress
17.	Smt. Uma Pandey	Congress
18.	Smt. Banarsasi Devi	Congress
19.	Smt. Sudama Choudhary	P.S.P.
20.	Smt. Ramdulari Shastri	Congress
21.	Smt. Krishna Devi	Congress
22.	Smt. Shanti Devi	Congress
23.	Smt. Ram Sukumari Devi	Congress
24.	Smt. Shyam Kumari	Congress
25.	Smt. Vishweshwari Devi	Congress
26.	Smt. Shanti Devi	Independence
27.	Smt. Parwati Devi	Congress
28.	Smt. Rani Jyotirmayee Devi	Congress
29.	Smt. Shailbala Roy	Congress
30.	Smt. Sarswati Devi	Congress

31.	Smt. Leela Devi	Congress
32.	Smt. Zahra Ahmad	Congress
33.	Smt. Manorama Devi	Congress
34.	Smt. Manorama Pandey	P.S.P.
35.	Smt. Sumitra Devi	Congress
36.	Smt. Rajkumari Devi	Congress
37.	Smt. Sashank Manjari	Janata
38.	Smt. Manorama Sinha	Congress
39.	Smt. Elsi Angeer	Nominated
	1962	
40.	Smt. Shakuntala Devi	Congress
41.	Smt. Rajkumari Devi	Congress
42.	Smt. Uma Pandey	Congress
43.	Smt. Sundari Devi	Congress
44.	Smt. Meera Devi	Congress
45.	Smt. Girija Devi	Congress
46.	Smt. Pratibha Devi	Congress
47.	Smt. Krishna Devi	Congress
48.	Sushri Shyam Kumari	Congress
49.	Smt. Ramsukumari Devi	Congress
50.	Smt. Shanti Devi	Congress
51.	Smt. Yasoda Devi	Congress
52.	Smt. Shailbala Roy	Congress
53.	Smt. Maya Devi	Congress
54.	Smt. Vindhwasini Devi	Congress
55.	Smt. Leela Devi	Congress
56.	Smt. Prema Devi	Congress
57.	Smt. Girish Kumari Singh	Congress
58.	Smt. Sarswati Choudhary	Congress
59.	Smt. Zehra Ahmad	Congress
60.	Smt. Manorama Devi	Congress
61.	Smt. Sumitra Devi	Congress
62.	Smt. Manorama Pandey	P.S.P.
63.	Smt. Rajkumari Devi	Congress
64.	Smt. Elsi Angier	Nominated

	1967	
65.	Smt. Uma Pandey	Congress
66.	Smt. Shyama Patel	Congress
67.	Smt. Pratibha Devi	Congress
68.	Smt. Premlata Rai	S.S.P.
69.	Sushri Shyam Kumari	Congress
70.	Smt. Yashoda Devi	Congress
71.	Smt. Sushila Kapoor	P.S.P.
72.	Smt. Sumitra Devi	Congress
73.	Smt. Shanti Devi	Congress
74.	Smt. Shashank Manjari	Jankranti
75.	Smt. Madhujyotsna Akhouri	Jankranti
76.	Smt. Elsi Angier	Nominated
	1969	
77.	Smt. Ramdulari Sinha	Congress
78.	Smt. Sunaina Devi	C.P.I.
79.	Smt. Bhagwati Devi	S.S.P.
80.	Smt. Shashank Manjari	Janata
	1972	
81.	Smt. Prabhawati Gupta	Congress
82.	Smt. Rajpati Devi	Congress
83.	Smt. Ramdulari Singh	Congress
84.	Smt. Ansuya Devi	Congress
85.	Smt. Uma Pandey	Congress
86.	Smt. Beula Doza	Congress
87.	Smt. Krishna Shahi	Congress
88.	Smt. Sumitra Devi	Congress
89.	Smt. Manorama Pandey	Congress
90.	Smt. Gayatri Devi	Congress
91.	Smt. Shahedun Nisa	C.P.I.
	1977	
92.	Smt. Prabhawati Gupta	Congress
93.	Smt. Radhika Devi	Janata
94.	Smt. Premlata Rai	Janata
95.	Smt. Veena Rani	Janata
96.	Smt. Sudha Srivastava	Janata

97.	Smt. Koshalya Devi	Janata
98.	Smt. Krishna Shahi	Congress
99.	Smt. Sumitra Devi	Janata
100.	Smt. Sushila Sahaya	Janata
101.	Smt. Rani De	Janata
102.	Smt. Muktidani Sumbrui	Jharkhand

Bihar Vidhan Sabha Election 1980
Women Winners

1.	Kamala Devi	Congress-I
2.	Prabhawati Gupta	Congress-I
3.	Uma Pandey	Congress-I
4.	Ram Sukumari Devi	Congress-I
5.	Beula Doza	Congress-I
6.	Prabhawati Singh	Congress-I
7.	Tara Gupta	Congress (U)
8.	Raj Kumari Devi	Congress-I
9.	Gayatri Devi	Congress-I
10.	Ramnika Gupta	Janata (S) (Charan Singh)
11.	Muktidani Simbrui	Independence

Source: Bihar Legislative Assembly Election 1980; A Statistical Analysis, Patna Superintendent, Secretariat Press 1983, pp. 228-231.

Women Winner 1985 Bihar Vidhan Sabha Elections

1.	Smt. Kamala Pandey	INC
2.	Smt. Uma Pandey	INC
3.	Smt. Usha Singh	LD
4.	Smt. Padma Chaube	INC
5.	Smt. Hemlata Yadav	INC
6.	Smt. Shakuntala Sinha	CPI
7.	Smt. Beula Doza	INC
8.	Smt. Rajmati Devi	INC
9.	Smt. Jyoti Devi	INC
10.	Smt. Shashi Rani Mishra	INC

11.	Smt. Sumitra Devi	INC
12.	Smt. Gayatri Devi	INC
13.	Smt. Lata Devi	INC
14.	Smt. Sushila Karketta	INC

Source: Bihar Vidhan Sabha General Elections 1985; A Statistical Analysis, Patna. Superintendent, Secretariat Press, 1086, pp. 109-11.

Bihar Vidhan Sabha Election 1990
Women Winners

1.	Smt. Veena Pandey	Congress-I
2.	Smt. Sushila Hansda	JMM
3.	Smt. Sudha Srivastava	JD
4.	Smt. Manju Prakash	CPM
5.	Smt. Jyoti	Congress-I
6.	Smt. Gayatri Devi	Congress-I
7.	Smt. Sushila Karketta	Congress-I
8.	Smt. Madhu Singh	IND
9.	Smt. Shanti Devi	JD

Saurce: The *Hindustan Times*, Patna Monday March 5, 1990, p. 4.

Bihar Vidhan Sabha Election 1995
Women Winners

1.	Smt. Sita Sinha	JD
2.	Smt. Shanti Devi	JD
3.	Smt. Kanti Singh	RJD
4.	Smt Abo Devi	JD
5.	Smt. Chandramukhi Devi	BJP
6.	Smt. Manju Prakash	CPM
7.	Smt. Sushila Hansada	JMM (S)
8.	Smt. Joba Manjhia	(Jharkhand Peoples Party)
9.	Smt. Sushila Karketta	Congress

Source: *Hindustan Paper*, 1995, 14 April, p. 8.

Bihar Vidhan Sabha Election 2000
Women Winners

1.	Smt. Bhagirathi Devi	BJP
2.	Smt. Renu Devi	BJP
3.	Smt. Rama Devi	RJD
4.	Smt. Kiran Devi	RJD
5.	Smt. Prema Chaudhary	RJD
6.	Smt. Veena Shahi	INC
7.	Smt. Ashwamegh Devi	SAP
8.	Smt. Geeta Devi	RJD
9.	Smt. Bimla Bharti	IND
10.	Smt. Lesha Devi	SAP
11.	Smt. Sushila Hansada	JMM
12.	Smt Sudha Srivastava	SAP
13.	Smt. Sukhda Pandey	BJP
14.	Smt. Bhagawati Devi	RJD
15.	Smt Gayatri Devi	RJD
16.	Smt. Aruna Devi	IND
17.	Smt. Annapura Devi	RJD
18.	Smt. Menka Sarda	BJP
19.	Smt. Joba Manjhi	UGDP

Source: General Elections to State Assembly 2000, pp. A 73-A 77.

APPENDIX-III: CHAPTER-1

Women Ministers in Bihar 1952-2001

2nd Ministry: 6.5.1957-31.1.1961

Sl.No.		*Name*	*Portfolio*
1.	Smt. Rani Jyotirmayu Devi	Dy. Minister	Welfare, Health
2.	Smt. Rageshwari Saroj Das	Dy. Minister	Forest, Tribal Welfare

3rd Ministry: 18.2.1961-14.3.1962

1.	Smt. Jyotirmayu Devi.	Dy. Minister	Health
2.	Smt. Rajeshwari Saroj Das	Dy. Minister	Forest & Tribal Welfare

5th Ministry: 15.3.1962-2.10.1963 (Parliamentary Secretary)

1.	Smt. Manorama Pandey		With Chief Minister
2.	Smt. Sumitra Devi		Health

5th Ministry: 2.10.1963-5.3.1967

1.	Smt. Sumitra Devi	Cabinet Minister	Information & Family Welfare

6th Ministry: 5.3.1967-28.1.1968

1.	Smt. Premlata Roy	Cabinet Minister	PHED & Family Welfare

7th Ministry: 2.6.1971-31.10.72

1.	Smt. Ram Dulari Sinha	Cabinet Minister	Labour, Employment, Social Welfare

16th Ministry: 19.3.1972-28.5.1972

1.	Smt. Ram Dulari Sinha	Cabinet Minister	Labour and Employment, Sugar, Tourism, Social Welfare
2.	Smt. Simla Doza	State Minister	Family Welfare
3.	Smt. Manorama Pandey	Dy. Minister	Home (Police), Public Relation

17th Ministry: 28.5.1972-2.7.1973

1.	Smt. Ram Dulari Sinha	Cabinet Minister	Labour & Employment
2.	Smt. Bimla Doza	State Minister	Social Welfare, Family Planning
3.	Smt. Manorama Pandey,	State Minister	Secondary & Higher Education

18th Ministry: 2.7.1973-11.4.1975

1.	Smt. Ram Dulari Sinha	Cabinet Minister	Labour, Employment, Tourism, Social Welfare
2.	Smt. Manorama Pandey	State Minister	Public Construction

19th Ministry

1.	Smt. Ram Dulari Sinha	Cabinet Minister	Labour & Employment

20th Ministry: 24.6.1977-21.4.1979

1.	Smt. Sumitra Devi	Cabinet Minister	N.A.
2.	Smt. Sushila Sahay	State Minister	Home
3.	Smt. Lalita Rajlaxmi,	State Minister	Finance

21st Ministry: 21.4.1970-17.2.1980

1.	Smt. Kaushalya Devi	State Minister	Public Construction

22nd Ministry: 8.6.1980-14.3.1983

1.	Smt. Uma Pandey	State Minister	Urban Development, Tourism
2.	Smt. Prabhawati Gupta	State Minister	Jail

24th Ministry: 12.3.1985-13.2.1988

1.	Smt. Uma Pandey	Cabinet Minister	Education, Rajbhasha, Science & Technology except Youth Welfare, Sports & Culture
2.	Smt. Sushila Kerketta	State Minister	Irrigation

25th Ministry: 14.2.1988-11.3.1989

1.	Smt. Uma Pandey	Cabinet Minister	Revenue, Land Reforms, Relief and Rehabilitation, Religious Trust
2.	Stencila Hembram	State Minister	Health and Family Welfare

26th Ministry: 11.3.1989-6.12.1989

1.	Smt. Sushila Kerketta	Cabinet Minister	Food & Civil Supply, Commerce, Rural Development
2.	Smt. Sumitra Devi	Cabinet Minister	Urban Development
3.	Smt. Gayatri Devi	State Minister	Animal Husbandry, Fisheries
4.	Smt. Jyoti	Dy. Minister	Education

27th Ministry: 6.12.1989-10.3.1990

1.	Smt. Sumitra Devi	Cabinet Minister	Urban Development
2.	Smt. Uma Pandey	Cabinet Minister	Human Resource, Rajbhasha
3.	Smt. Sushila Kerketta	Cabinet Minister	Mines and Geology
4.	Smt. Jyoti	State Minister	Co-operative, Transport

28th Ministry: 10.3.1990-14.4.1995

1.	Smt. Sudha Srivastava	Cabinet Minister	Health (except Medical Education and Family Welfare)
2.	Smt. Shanti Devi	Dy. Minister	Transport

29th Ministry: 4.4.1995-24.7.1997

1.	Smt. Shanti Devi	Cabinet Minister	Sugar Cane

30th Ministry: 25.7.1997-11.2.1999

1.	Mrs. Rabri Devi	Cabinet Minister	Cabinet Secretariat & Coordination, Home

			(excepting Jail), Personnel Administration, Welfare, Civil Aviation (31.7.1997)
2.	Smt. Shanti Devi	Cabinet Minister	Transport
3.	Smt. Abo Devi	State Minister	Rural Development
4.	Smt. Sita Sinha	State Minister	Welfare (excluding Tribal Welfare)

***31st Ministry:* 8.3.1999-3.3.2000**

1.	Smt. Rabri Devi	Cabinet Minister	Cabinet Secretariat & Coordination, Home (excepting Jail), Personnel Administrative Reforms, Welfare, Civil Aviation
2.	Smt. Shanti Devi	Cabinet Minister	Transport
3.	Smt. Abo Devi	State Minister	Rural Development
4.	Smt. Sita Sinha	State Minister	Welfare (excluding Scheduled Castes)

33rd Ministry: 11.3.2000-

1.	Smt. Rabri Devi	Cabinet Minister	Cabinet Secretariat & Coordination, Home (excepting Jail), Administrative Reforms, Finance (ex-Commercial Taxes & Rural National Savings), Planning, Weight & Measurement, Horticulture, Civil Aviation, Minority Welfare.
2.	Smt. Veena Shahi	Cabinet Minister	Co-operative
3.	Mrs. Rama Devi	Cabinet Minister	PHED
4.	Smt. Annapurna Devi	State Minister	Mines & Mineral (till 15.1 1.2000)
5.	Smt. Joba Manjhi	State Minister	N.A. (till 5.11.2000)

APPENDIX-III CHAPTER-1

Women in Council of Ministers Centre (From Bihar) 1947

Year	*Name of the Women Minister*	*Rank*			*Portfolios*
		Cabinet Minister	*State Minister*	*Deputy Minister*	
1958	Smt. Tarkeshwari Sinha	—	—	Do	Economic Affairs
1959-1961	Smt. Tarkeshwari Sinha	—	—	Do	Finance
1962-1863	Smt. Tarkeshwari Sinha	—	—	Do	Finance
1966	Smt. Jahanara Jaipal Singh	—	—	Do	Transport & Aviation
1962-1968	Smt. Jahanara Jaipal Singh	—	—	Do	Tourism & Civil Aviation
1969	Smt. Jahanara Jaipal Singh	—	—	Do	Education & Youth Services
1980	Smt. Ram Dulari Sinha	—	Do	—	Information and Broadcasting
	Kr. Kamla Kumari	—	—	Do	Agriculture
1981	Smt. Ram Dulari Sinha	—	Do	—	Labour
	Kr. Kamla Kumari	—	—	Do	Agriculture
1982(I)	Kr. Kamala Kumari	—	—	Do	Health & Family Welfare
1982(II)	Smt. Ram Dulari Sinha	—	Do	—	Industry, Steel & Mines
	Kr. Kamala Kumari	—	—	Do	Agriculture
1983	Smt. Ram Dulari Sinha	—	Do	—	Commerce
1984	Smt. Ram Dulari Sinha	—	Do	—	Home Ministry
1985	Smt. Ram Dulari Sinha	—	Do	—	Youth Affairs/Sports/ Women
1986-1989	Smt. Krishna Shahi	—	Do	—	Minister for Education & Culture State Minister for Water Resources & Culture
1996-98	Smt. Kanti Singh	—	Do	—	Minister of State for Coal
1999	Smt. Rita Verma	Do	—	—	

Source: Councils of Ministers in India, 1947-82.

APPENDIX-I TO CHAPTER-III

Work Participation by Gender in Bihar-1911-1961

Year	Total Population	Total Workers	Cultivators	Agricultural Labourers	Plantations Forestry, Fishing, Livestock & Housing	Mining and Quarrying	Manufacturing Including Household Industry	Construction	Trade and Commerce	Transport, Storage and Communication	Other Services	Unclassified & General Labour
1	2	3	4	5	6	7	8	9	10	11	12	13
BIHAR						PERSONS						
1911	28,316,916	13,681,740	7108.415	3,427,708	469,468	32,173	743,201	76,106	664,052	121,271	685,158	354,189
1921	28,129,208	13,928,648	8,797,497	2,444,194	253,752	50,593	634,163	48,943	511,923	62,693	529,645	595,245
1931	31,349,892	12,995,305	7,448,662	2,698,722	173,419	34,442	548,268	46,162	422,202	59,539	448,364	1,115,525
1951	38,786,184	13,565,176	8,147,682	3,238,407	89,346	163,797	459,824	61,884	510,418	133,027	448,438	312,353
1961	46,455,610	19,234,565	10,361,971	4,418,475	537,385	271,225	1,327,369	108,342	522,949	230,543	840,914	615,392
						MALES						
1911	13,855,597	8,662,642	5,039,231	1,725,581	335,323	14,952	413,953	50,954	355,463	115,178	396,756	185,251
1921	13,955,184	8,834,968	5,885,944	1,280,487	214,027	28,104	380,814	34,227	289,054	60,528	344,643	317,140
1931	15,725,848	8,918,112	5,551,863	1,499,569	145,040	22,537	372,888	34,327	275,793	58,344	289,215	668,836
1951	19,491,817	9,575,261	5,779,484	2,143,568	67,597	133,929	331,511	49,946	374,395	113,809	335,799	245,233
1961	23,301,449	12,955,469	6,926,037	2,574,239	429,041	227,148	873,676	99,333	448,487	227,763	720,614	429,051

FEMALES

1911	14,461,019	5,019,098	2,039,184	1,702,127	1,34,145	17,221	329,248	25,151	308,589	6,093	288,402	168,938
1921	14,174,024	5,093,680	2,911,553	1,163,707	39,725	22,489	253,349	14,716	222,869	2,165	185,002	278,105
1931	15,624,044	4,076,893	1,896,799	1,199,153	28,379	11,905	175,380	11,835	146,409	1,195	159,149	446,689
1951	19,294,367	3,989,915	2,368,198	1,094,839	21,759	29,868	128,313	11,938	136,023	19,218	112,639	67,120
1961	23,154,161	6,279,156	3,435,914	1,844,236	108,344	44,077	453,693	9,009	74,462	2,780	120,300	186,341

Source: Census of India 1961 paper no. 1 of 1967; subsidiarytables B-I.6 and B-II.3, New Delhi, Registrar General & Census Commission, 1968, p. 6.

Work Participation by Gender in Bihar-1971-1991

Year	Total Population	Total Workers	Cultivators	Agricultural Labourers	Livestock Forestry, etc.	Mining and Quarrying	Household Industry	Other than Household	Construction	Trade and Commerce	Transfer, Commmnication	Other services
1	2	3	4	5	6	7	8	9	10	11	12	13
PERSONS												
1971	56,353,369											
1981		20,753,128	9,042,045	7,366,973	X	X		495,124				
1991		25,619,038	11,164,519	9,512,892	99,444	322,741	447,008	578,537	962,230	1,024,837	328,925	1,977,905
MALES												
1971		15,047,304	7,155,142	4,008,881	159,621	232,567	373,005	434,098	92,357	548,598	258,779	783,256
1981		17,615,805	8,256,140	5,418,023	X	X	410,220	X	X	X	X	3,596,422
1991		21,513,704	9,867,434	7,078,716	91,604	300,485	360,300	540,347	153,726	988,960	324,997	1,807,395
FEMALES												
1971		2,441,575	423,556	1,797,222	8,962	25,899	59,587	10,504	5,789	21,604	6,007	72,445
1981		3,077,323	785,945	1,948,950	X	X	84,404	X	X	X	X	257,522
1991		4,105,334	1,297,085	2,434,176	7,840	22,256	86,708	38,190	8,504	35,937	4,128	170,510

N.B.: Industrial Category for the Census year 1981 and 1991 is based only on main workers.

Source: (i) Census of India 1971 Series I-India Part ii (B) I General Economic Tables, New Delhi, Manager of Publications. 1977 pp. 24-25.

(ii) Census of India 1981 Series I India Part ii (B)l; Primary Census Abstract-General Population, New Delhi, Manager of Publication, 1983, pp. 62-64.

(iii) Census of India 1991 Series I-India, Final Population Totals; Brief Analysis of Primary Census Abstract, 1992, pp. 128-129.

A.B. Kohli, Gitanjali Publishing House, New Delhi, 1983.

APPENDIX-II TO CHAPTER-III

Massacres in Bihar 1977-2000

Sl. No.	*Year*	*Village*	*District*	*No. of dead*	*Caste*
1.	1977	Dharmpura	Bhojpur	4	Dalit
2.	1977	Belchchi	Patna	14	Dalit
3.	1977	Brahampur	Bhojpur	4	Dalit
4.	1979	Samghita	Rohtas	4	Dalit
5.	1980	Pipra	Patna	14	Dalit
6.	1981	Parasbigha	Jehanabad	11	Dalit
7.	1984	Gaganbigha	Rohtas	5	Dalit
8.	1985	Laxmipur	Munger	12	OBC
9.	1986	Maini	Aurangabad	12	Dalit
10.	1986	Arwal	Jehanabad	27	Dalit
11.	1986	Kansara	Jehanabad	15	Dalit
12.	1986	Parasdiha	Rohtas	17	OBC
13.	1987	Parmia	Aurangabad	11	Upper Caste
14.	1987	Chechani	Aurangabad	7	OBC
15.	1987	Dalelchak	Aurangabad	56	Upper Caste
16.	1988	Nanhi Nagwan	Jehanabad	19	Dalit
17.	1988	Demuha Khagdi	Jehanabad	11	Dalit
18.	1988	Galakpur	Jehanabad	4	Dalit
19.	1988	Tarahi	Jehanabad	4	Dalit
20.	1988	Koderia	Jehanabad	7	OBC
21.	1989	Tijopur	Rohtas	6	Dalit
22.	1986	Malibigha	Jehanabad	5	Upper Caste
23.	1990	Kanosari	Rohtas	10	Dalit
24.	1990	Lakhawar	Jehanabad	5	Dalit
25.	1990	Dariapur	Patna	4	Dalit
26.	1991	Teeskhora	Patna	14	Dalit
27.	1991	Melbaria	Palamu	11	Dalit
28.	1991	Deosariara	Bhojpur	14	Dalit
29.	1991	Sawabigha	Jehanabad	7	Dalit
30.	1991	Menbarsinha	Jehanabad	9	Dalit
31.	1991	Karkatbigha	Patna	4	Dalit

32.	1991	Teendiha	Gaya	7	OBC
33.	1992	Bara	Gaya	39	Upper Caste
34.	1993	Ekhari	Bhojpur	4	Dalit
35.	1994	Nahi	Bhojpur	9	Dalit
36.	1994	Mathanbigha	Bhojpur	11	Dalit
37.	1995	Khopira	Bhojpur	3	Dalit
38.	1995	Sathua	Bhojpur	6	Dalit
39.	1995	Nonur	Bhojpur	6	Dalit
40.	1996	Chandi	Bhojpur	4	
41.	1996	Patalpura	Bhojpur	3	
42.	1996	Monaur	Bhojpur	5	
43.	1996	Nadhi	Bhojpur	3	Dalit
44.	1996	Nadhi	Bhojpur	3	Dalit
45.	1996	Nadhi	Bhojpur	3	Dalit
46.	1996	Morath	Bhojpur	3	
47.	1996	Bathanitola	Bhojpur	21	Dalit
48.	1996	Purhara	Bhojpur	4	
49.	1996	Khaner	Bhojpur	6	Dalit
50.	1996	Ekhari	Bhojpur	6	Dalit
51.	1997	Raghopur	Patna	9	Upper Caste
52.	1997	Hasanpura	Patna	10	Dalit
53.	1997	Laxmanpur Bathe	Jehanabad	61	Dalit
54.	1997	Rampura Chauran	Jehanabad	9	Upper Caste
55.	1998	Atkadiha	Palamu	10	OBC
56.	1998	Nikhral	Purnia	20	Tribal
57.	1998	Nagdi	Bhojpur	10	Dalit
58.	1998	Khadasin	Jehanabad	8	Dalit
59.	1999	Shankarbigha	Jehanabad	23	Dalit
60.	1999	Mipura	Jehanabad	4	Upper Caste
61.	1999	Narayanpur	Jehanabad	11	Dalit
62.	1999	Senari	Jehanabad	34	Upper Caste
63.	1999	Khagdi bigha	Gaya	12	Dalit
64.	2000	Rajabigha	Nawada	5	Yadav & Bhumihar
65.	2000	Baghi	Nawada	3	Kurmi-Bhumihar
66	12.6.00	Aksar	Nawada	13	Bhumihar-Yadav
67.	14.10.00	Bhojpur	Nawada	5	Backward Bhumihar

68.	14.10.00	Mojahidpur	Siwan	13	Backward Bhumihar
69.	18.10.00	Vishwanathpur	Nawada	4	Backward Bhumihar

Sources:

1. *Hindustan* 13 February, 1999
2. *Hindustan* 13 March, 1999
3. *Hindustan Times* 12 February, 1999
4. *India Today* 22 February, 1999, p. 26
5. *Hindustan* 19 March, 1999
6. *Hindustan Times* 24 April, 1999
7. *Hindustan Times* 16 October, 2000
8. *Hindustan Times* 19 October, 2000

APPENDIX-III-CHAPTER-III

Criminals in the Fray-Assembly Elections 2000

1.	Rama Singh	Mahnar	JD (U)
2.	Arvind Singh	Ichagarh	BJP
3.	Ram Lakhan Singh	Barauni	BJP
4.	Satish Pandey	Drauli	Samata
5.	Sunil Pandey	Piro	Samata
6.	Bachcha Singh	Jharia	Samata
7.	Sarfaraj Alam	Jokhihatt	RJD
8.	Surendra Yadav	Belganj	RJD
9.	Raj Ballabh Yadav	Nawada	RJD
10.	Dilip Singh	Mokama	JD
11.	Rakesh Choudhary	Parbatta	RJD
12.	Upendra Singh	Ichagarh	Congress
13.	Vijay Singh Soy	Kharswan	Congress
14.	Syed Naushad	Jamshedpur	JMM (S)
15.	Banna Gupta	Jamshedpur	JMM (Marandi)
16.	Dulal Bhiya	Jugsalari	JMM (S)
17.	Krishna Mardi	Potka	JMM (S)
18.	Manoranjan Singh	Baniapur	Independent
19.	Suraj Bhan Singh	Mokama	Independent
20.	Rajan Tiwari	Govindganj	Independent
21.	Vijay Kumar Shukla	Lalganj	Independent
22.	Captain Sunil	Patna	Indpendent
23.	Bootan Singh	Dhamdaha	Independent
24.	Pappu Deo	Sipri	Independent
25.	Tikker Singh	Barhaiya	Independent
26.	Bablu Deo	Madhuban	Independent
27.	Dularchand Yadav	Barh	Independent
28.	Sardar Krishna	Arwal	Independent
29.	Sattan Yadav	Nautan	Independent
30.	Ram Bhajju Yadav	Ram Nagar	Independent
31.	Satish Chandra Dubey	Chanpatia	Independent

Source: Outlook-The Art of Survival dated 14 February, 2000.

APPENDIX-1 CHAPTER-7

List of MLA Respondents

1.	Shakuntala Sinha	Ex-MLA	CPI
2.	Annapurna Devi	MLA	RJD
3.	Manorama Singh	Ex-MLA	Congress
4.	Chandramukhi Devi	Ex-MLA	BJP
5.	Shyama Patel	Ex-MLA	Congress
6.	Hemlata Yadav	Ex-MLA	RJD
7.	Bina Rani	Ex-MLA	JD
8.	Vaidehi Devi	Ex-MLA	Congress
9.	Veena Vadini Devi	Ex-MLA	Congress
10.	Prabhawati Singh	Ex-MLA	Samata
11.	Manju Prakash	Ex-MLA	CPI
12.	Madhavi Sarkar	Ex-MLA	CPM
13.	Sushila Kerketta	Ex-MLA	Congress
14.	Sushila Hansda	MLA	JMM
15.	Jova Manjhi	MLA	MGDP
16.	Poonam Devi	Ex-MLA	Congress
17.	Tara Gupta	Ex-MLA	Samajwadi Party
18.	Parvati Devi	Ex-MLA	Samata
19.	Manorama Pandey	Ex-MLA	Congress
20.	Anusuya Jaiswal	Ex-MLA	Congress
21.	Seema Devi	Ex-MLA	RJD
22.	Veena Shahi	MLA	Congress
23.	Lovely Anand	Ex-MLA	BPP
24.	Urmila Devi	Ex-MLA	Congress

List of Ministers. Ex-Minister's Respondent

1.	Tarkeshwari Sinha	Ex-Minister	Congress
2.	Uma Pandey	Ex-Minister	Congress
3.	Prabhawati Gupta	Ex-Minister	Congress
4.	Kumari Jyoti	Ex-Minister	Congress
5.	Abo Devi	Ex-Minister	RJD
6.	Shanti Devi	Ex-Minister	RJD
7.	Sita Sinha	Ex-Minister	RJD
8.	Gayatri Devi	Ex-Minister	Congress
9.	Kamla Sinha	Ex-Minister	JD
10.	Sudha Srivastava	Ex-Minister	BJP
11.	Rama Devi	Ex-Minister	RJD
12.	Usha Singh	Minister	JD
13.	Manorama Pandey		Congress I

List of MLC Respondents

1.	Dr. Padmasha Jha	MLC	BJP
2.	Pramila Devi	MLC	RJD
3.	Silwiya Bage	MLC	Congress
4.	Bibha Ranjan		Congress I
5.	Kalawati Tripathi	Ex-MLC	Congress
6.	Indu Singh	MLC	RJD

List of MP Respondents

1.	Shakuntala Devi	Ex-MP	Congress I
2.	Krishna Shahi	Ex-MP	Congress I
3.	Kanti Singh	MP	RJD
4.	Bhagwati Devi	Ex-MP	JD
5.	Malti Devi	Ex-MP	RJD
6.	Girija Devi	Ex-MP	JD
7.	Saroj Dubey	MP	RJD
8.	Kishori Sinha	Ex-MP	Congress I

Index

■■■